Protecting Your Family in Dangerous Times

BY

KELLIE COPELAND KUTZ

Harrison House
Tulsa, Oklahoma

06 05 04 03   10 9 8 7 6 5

Protecting Your Family in Dangerous Times
ISBN 1-57794-272-8
Copyright © 2002 by Kellie Copeland Kutz
Fort Worth, Texas 76192-0001

Published by Harrison House, Inc.
P. O. Box 35035
Tulsa, Oklahoma 74153

Printed in the United States of America.

This book is dedicated to my family.

To Win, Rachel, Lyndsey, Jenny and Max

Contents

Acknowledgments

Thank you, Win, for being the man of God that you are and for your encouragement and strength. Rachel, Lyndsey, Jenny and Max—I thank you for being all that a mother could dream of in her children. Thank you for being obedient and pleading the blood of Jesus every day.

I want to thank you, Mother and Daddy, for teaching me the Word and living a life of faith before me. Because of you, I trust in God.

And, the rest of my family (you know who you are), thank you for your support, for prayer and for believing in me.

Especially to my Pastors—thank you, Terri and George, for everything.

To Billye Brim, I must give a hearty thank you. I'm grateful to you for starting me on this journey and teaching me about the blood.

Thank you, Jerry and Carolyn Savelle, for JSMI and for being there every time I need you.

To the Harrison House staff—especially Becky, Mona and Naomi—thank you for your patience and help. I needed you.

To Lisa Flanagain—you are a dream assistant. Thank you for typing, for keeping me organized and for checking my email.

Most of all, thank You, Jesus, for Your precious blood and thank You for seeing to it that I don't miss out on anything that You have for me.

Love and thanks to all,

Kellie Copeland Kutz

Foreword

By Kenneth Copeland

The shed blood of Jesus is the fullness of love expressed—holding out its offer of salvation to the extreme—divine protection from sin, sickness, demons, fear and hell in the end and heaven in the beginning. It is heaven's guarantee on the earth that all God has promised is divinely true. True to any and everyone who will accept it so that all may walk in its glorious protection and holy prosperity. Think about it. The spotless, pure, sinless, holy, righteous blood of almighty God—Love Himself—poured out for the likes of you and me! Read this book thinking about it. Read a couple of chapters and then stop and meditate on it again.

This is a very important book for this dangerous hour in which we live. Read it until fear is flushed out of your life like a covey of birds flushed out of their hiding places and rushing away before your face. God loves you! He poured out His life for you. He swore every promise of His holy Word directly to you in His own blood on the cross. Receive it. Take your place as His very own love child. Cry out of your heart from the spirit of adoption—"I have a Father! He's mine and I'm His! He is The Most High God and He's my Father. I know Him and He knows me. I have it in writing in His own blood. There is no greater love than the way He loves me."

The Spirit of God has inspired Kellie to bring this message to us and has anointed her to share parts of her life with us. Read it and live it with her as you read.

May God richly bless and keep you.
JESUS IS LORD!
Kenneth Copeland

Introduction

God is so gracious to give us exactly what we need, just when we need it. I believe this book is one of those gifts. I know when He began to reveal these things to me, that was exactly how I felt. I knew that I had been given a precious gift—a deeper understanding of the protection of the blood of Jesus.

As I began my final edits on this book, the world and America as we knew it were changed in one tragic moment on September 11, 2001. It was more than just an attack on our nation—it was a direct assault on God and on His people. I began to realize that God wants people to know that we can trust Him with our whole life, and more importantly, with our family.

As I prayed about whether or not to add things concerning war, terrorism and biological threats, I felt that He wanted me to leave it the way He had given it to me. He knew what we would face in these days and He has everything we need to see us through. Praise God, even though the world may change, God's Word will not. He wants us to lay hold of all that He has for us and go forward in victory over the enemy!

Let me add one final thought before you begin this book. In reflecting on the changes in our lives since we began to plead the blood of Jesus eight years ago, I realized that fear had been eradicated in our family. The blood of Jesus has wiped it out! Do you realize that in any battle you face, fear will cause you to lose? In fear, we say the wrong things and do the wrong things. But when you begin to plead the blood of Jesus faith is built up and fear loses its grip on you. In the absence of fear you make the right decisions and you speak the Word of God and victory is yours!

I am very thankful to my Jesus, not only for His blood, but also for opening my eyes to real life in Him.

Kellie Copeland Kutz

CHAPTER 1

Make Sure Your Children Are Fully *Protected*

As a parent, you probably know only too well that overriding desire to protect your children from harm. You deal with that desire every time you send your children out the door to school or watch your teenagers drive off with their friends to the mall or to the movie.

But what goes through your mind in those moments when your children leave home for another day's activities? Just how sure are you that God will bring them home safely? Do you know with absolute confidence that the blood of Jesus will protect and deliver your children from every danger the world can throw at them that day?

Developing that rock-solid confidence is the goal you should be aiming for as a parent. But how do you reach that goal? What can you do as a parent to ensure that your children are protected every moment of every day?

A Wake-up Call

I really began seeking the Lord about how to protect my children after my cousin Nikki died in a car accident. Nikki was Miss "On Fire for God," one of the most phenomenal people I have ever known. She had gone to Bible school in Sweden and was about the boldest thing on two feet you have ever seen!

Nikki didn't mince any words with people. She was just very bold about speaking out her faith, a real powerhouse for God.

But several years ago, Nikki's life was suddenly snuffed out. The day before our Southwest Believers' Convention, she was killed in a car accident involving a drunk driver.

Nikki's death was a huge wake-up call to me. Now, I would never question God by saying, "Why did You let this happen?" I did, however, pray, "Lord, I want You to show me how we let this happen. What do we need to do to make sure it never happens again?"

God began to answer that prayer immediately. The same week that Nikki died a close friend and anointed minister named Billye Brim, who teaches on the blood of Jesus, stressed to me that, "We have to plead the blood of Jesus over our families every morning and every night."

It was the first time I had heard that we needed to do that. It was such a profound revelation to me! I thought, *I don't know what she's talking about—but I'm going to find out!* (Billye has written a wonderful book on this subject that I recommend to everyone. It's called *The Blood and the Glory.*)

From that time on, I started to plead the blood of Jesus over my children every day just because Billye told me to. Later Billye came to our church and taught us about the blood of Jesus in more depth. And as I began to walk in what I had learned, the Lord began to teach me more.

You see, I'm the type of person who likes to know *why* things work. So I began to study the Word on the subject. Once I learned more about the power in the blood, I didn't need anyone else to prompt me. I determined to *daily* claim the protection of the blood of Jesus over my children for the rest of my life! Now, it took some time to build a habit and lifestyle, but once you understand *why* we need to plead the blood, it's easy to make the decision to do it.

I'm so grateful to the Lord for opening my eyes to His protection. And, as trouble escalates in the world I realize more and more what a priceless gift God has given me. Today I can send my children out the door to their daily activities, knowing with absolute certainty that they will be safe. I can let my teenage daughters get behind the wheel of our car and drive off, knowing that, no matter what, they are protected and will come home safely.

What a gift that is! And the wonderful thing is that you don't have to take as long as I did to enjoy that gift. You can begin operating in the truths presented in this book today!

Take Advantage of Angelic Protection

Pleading the blood of Jesus is the main thing God taught me pertaining to divine protection after Nikki's death. However, before I go on to share what He taught me about the blood, I want to mention three other truths He taught me that must be operating in your life if your children are to be fully protected. I want to make sure every area of your life is covered according to the Word.

First, you have to *understand and appropriate the angelic ministry.* Angels are servants sent to minister for you. The world has made them little gods or icons, but the truth is, they are *servants.* More importantly, they are *your* servants.

According to Hebrews 2:5-6 AMP, angels are not placed higher than you spiritually:

> **For it was not to angels that God subjected the habitable world of the future, of which we are speaking. It has been solemnly and earnestly said in a certain place, What is man that You are mindful of him, or the son of man that You graciously and helpfully care for and visit and look after him?**

We may seem insignificant when we compare ourselves to angels. But God doesn't see it that way. He sent His angels to helpfully care for and look after us!

Hebrews 1:14 says, **Are they not all ministering spirits, sent forth to minister for them who shall be heirs of salvation?** The "them" in that verse is talking about us. *We* are the heirs of salvation, and the angels have been sent to minister for us! That means we have been given the authority to tell the angels what to do according to the Word.

Therefore, you need to understand how to send your angels about their business of ministering for you. You also need to understand how *not* to mess up what they are trying to do for you with careless words of doubt and unbelief!

I once read a book by Charles Capps entitled *Angels* that greatly helped me in this regard. I grew up learning how to speak the Word and avoid speaking negative things, but this book made me pay even more attention to my words than I had before.

Charles Capps' book will cause you to restrain your lips from speaking negatively—to just be quiet, if that's what it takes. It will also teach you how to begin speaking right things so your angels can do what they need to do for you.

For example, suppose you keep telling your child, "Don't go out in the street, or a car will hit you." Now, an opportunity may never arise in your child's life to run out in the street at the same time a car is driving past. But if that situation ever did arise, the angels would only be able to act according to the words of your mouth.

According to what you've been saying, your will is that the approaching car would hit your child, who should have heeded your words and stayed out of the street. Thus, your angels have to fold their hands. They can't rescue your child or keep the car from hitting him because that is what you've been saying.

God has given you the authority to command the angels to act on your behalf. Therefore, it is very important that you watch what comes out of your mouth. Make sure that your words reflect what you want to come to pass because your angels were created to obey what you say.

So charge the angels to go forth on your behalf. Say, "I charge you angels, in the Name of Jesus, to watch over my children today, to go before them to protect them and keep them from all harm!" Then make sure you don't speak any negative words that bind the angels' hands from helping you!

Listen to Your Spirit

Another thing the Lord dealt with me about after Nikki died is that *you have to learn to listen to your spirit*. This is so important. You can't protect your children if you haven't learned to discern what the Spirit of God is saying to you. (Two of the best books that can help you along this line are entitled *To Know Him* and *Hearing from Heaven*. Both are authored by my mother, Gloria Copeland, who is well skilled in listening to her own spirit.)

You see, God is always speaking to us. I don't believe one calamity ever happens to us that the Holy Spirit didn't speak to our spirits beforehand to warn us.

John 16:13 says that the Spirit of truth will show us things to come. He knows what the enemy is trying to do. But we have to learn to pick up on what He is saying so we can obey Him. If we are in tune to His voice, He can protect us from the devil's attacks on our lives.

There have certainly been times in my life when I have failed to heed the Holy Spirit's warning. When certain negative things have happened to me or my family, I've been able to look back and see that the Holy Spirit nudged me to go a different way or to do something I didn't do.

But I finally prayed, "Lord, I want to learn how to hear Your voice. I want to know exactly what Your voice sounds like so that when You are speaking to me, I will pick up on it." I'm telling you, God took me to school after I prayed that prayer! He put me through one little exercise after another, and His training caused me to grow light years in my spiritual walk!

If you've never prayed that prayer, I strongly suggest that you do it. All you have to do is say, "Lord, I want to be able to hear You when You speak to me. I want to know what You sound like."

I promise you, God will answer that prayer and start teaching you through simple little lessons. During the day, you'll hear something on the inside and you'll think, *Was that God?* Then after you either act on His prompting or ignore it, He'll come right behind it and prove to you that it *was* His voice you heard. As Isaiah 30:21 AMP says, **Your ears will hear a word behind you, saying, This is the way; walk in it.**

How can you be sure that God will teach you how to hear what He is saying to you? Proverbs 3:5-6 tells you: **Trust in the Lord with all thine heart; and lean not unto thine own understanding. In all thy ways acknowledge him, and he shall direct thy paths.** When you ask the Lord to teach you how to discern His voice, you are acknowledging that He knows more than you do. And because you are acknowledging Him, He will begin to direct your paths.

First Peter 5:8 tells you to be *sober* and *vigilant.* That is also a part of listening to the Spirit of God. Keep your spiritual antenna up, always listening on the inside for the Holy Spirit's leading. Stay vigilant to plead the blood of Jesus over your children and to pray for them every day.

Be ever watchful because the enemy walks about as a roaring lion, seeking whom he may devour. But as you listen to your spirit and heed the Holy Spirit's voice, you can make sure he never has the opportunity to devour you or your family!

Discipline Your Children

I want to point out one more thing the Lord taught me when I asked Him to show me how to keep my children protected. He told me, "If you want your children to be protected, you will have to *discipline* them."

There's no way around it. The Word says that if your children are going to live long on the earth, they have to obey their parents. (Ephesians 6:1-3.) That doesn't just happen automatically. You have to teach them to be obedient, and the only way to do that is to *discipline* them.

You know, "discipline" is an ugly word to many people in today's society. Sadly, many Christians have bought into the world's idea of discipline.

The world says that if you discipline your children, they are going to turn against you and hate you. But actually, the exact opposite is true.

God laid out the perfect system in His Word for disciplining your children. Interestingly, He doesn't even mention "time-outs"! Actually, the only form of parental discipline the Word really talks about is spanking—and that's the one kind of discipline the world says *not* to use! Interesting, huh? (I recommend that you read Charles Sturgeon's book *Train Up Your Child*. It is an excellent book on how to scripturally discipline your children.)

What amazes me is that so many believers have agreed with the world on this subject of discipline. They say, "Well, the Bible is outdated in its instructions on discipline. Spanking a child is too violent." Not surprisingly, these Christians are also reaping the same results in their children that the world does—disobedience, disrespect and rebellion!

I haven't found any truth in the Bible that has passed away, and that includes God's instructions on parental discipline. It's important that we learn to discipline our children *God's* way.

Some people say, "Well, I am praying that my children will be obedient and not stray from the Word; therefore, I don't have to spank them."

But you can't believe God for something apart from the instruction in His Word. You have to obey what His Word says; only then are you in a position to believe God for the desired results—children who grow up to be obedient, respectful, a lot of fun—and continually protected from all harm!

This same principle applies not only to discipline, but also to the other prerequisites for divine protection that I've shared with you. First, you must obey what the Word tells you to do: plead the blood of Jesus over your children; utilize the angelic ministry on their behalf; learn how to listen to your spirit; and discipline your children consistently according to the Word. Then you can confidently expect what God has promised in His Word—continual supernatural protection for your family!

CHAPTER 2

Applying the Blood:
From Passover to Present

As you seek to develop a steadfast confidence in God's protection of your children, nothing is more important than building up your faith in the power resident within the blood of Jesus. The best place I know to start that process is the book of Exodus. This is where the Lord instituted a vital principle of protection that would forever remain one of His foundational truths: *deliverance from death and destruction through sacrificial blood.*

The book of Exodus tells us what happened as God worked through Moses to set His people free from their bondage in the land of Egypt. Throughout the entire ordeal, God protected the children of Israel from the plagues that were devastating the land around them.

Then in Exodus 12, God instituted the Passover to protect the Israelites from the final judgment on the people of Egypt: the death angel's visit to every firstborn in the land.

I'm sure the Israelites didn't understand exactly what was going on. Nevertheless, in Exodus 12:3 God instituted a requirement they would have to fulfill in order to experience this divine protection. God instructed Moses, **In the tenth day of this month they shall take to them every man a lamb, according to the house of their fathers, a lamb for an house.** *Every Israelite house had to have a lamb.*

Thank God, we have a Lamb as well! He's the matchless, precious Lamb of God, Jesus Christ. God appointed Jesus to be the Lamb for *our* house.

Keeping an Eternal Memorial by Pleading the Blood

In Exodus 12:14, the Lord went on to say something quite profound: **And this day shall be unto you for a memorial; and ye shall keep it a feast to the Lord throughout your generations; ye shall keep it a feast by an ordinance for ever.**

One thing I've noticed about God is that whenever He says something is to be kept as a memorial in the Old Testament, He gives the Church some way to keep that eternal ordinance under the New Covenant. He doesn't ask us to follow the natural instructions He gave the Israelites, but He does ask us to do something in the spiritual realm to keep His memorial.

So let's first see what some of God's original instructions were for the Passover feast. In Exodus 12:7, He said, **And they shall take of the blood, and strike it on the two side posts and on the upper door post of the houses, wherein they shall eat it.**

God told His people to apply the blood of the lamb with a hyssop branch to the doorposts of their house (v. 22). He instructed them to do this as a memorial unto Him forever. The Israelites kept this divine ordinance in the flesh, but how do we keep it as an eternal memorial under the New Covenant? We keep it in the Spirit by *pleading the blood of Jesus.*

The hyssop branch represents our faith. By faith we apply the blood of Jesus to the "doorposts" of our lives with our spoken words. That's the way we daily institute the Passover as an eternal memorial in our lives.

What Does It Mean to 'Plead the Blood'?

We need to continually be aware of our spiritual responsibility to plead the blood of Jesus over our children. "But

what does it mean to 'plead'?" you may ask. "I don't understand. That sounds like begging."

No, I'm not talking about begging God for anything. The
word "plead" is a legal term, as when you're standing in
court as a defendant in a legal case, and the judge asks,
"What is your plea—guilty or not guilty?" In the world's
court systems, those are the only two choices you have. But
in the high court of heaven, you can declare according to the
Word, "I plead the blood!"

The Bible says that the enemy is the accuser of the
brethren. (Revelation 12:10.) Daily he has his finger in your
face, trying to accuse you of something, trying his best to get
at you or your family in order to bring harm and destruction.

But when the accuser stands before the Judge of heaven
and says, "This person is guilty," you can say, "No, I am *not*
guilty. You can't harm me. This is not mine to take because
I'm not standing on my own righteousness. I am standing on
the shed blood of Jesus. He paid the price for me. Therefore,
I receive His righteousness. I receive His wholeness. I receive
His health, His wealth and His well-being."

That's what you're saying when you say, "I plead the
blood." You're saying, "I am innocent by the blood of Jesus.
You can't touch me, devil!"

When you plead the blood as your defense, it doesn't
matter if you're guilty or not guilty. The devil has to pass over!

The truth is, you can always find something to feel guilty about. But even if you are guilty, repent. The devil can't get to you when you plead the blood of Jesus.

In a courtroom, the prosecutor can't do anything to a defendant whom the judge declares innocent. Well, the Judge of all has declared you innocent by the blood of Jesus, and the prosecutor—the accuser of the brethren—can't do a thing about it.

One word of caution here: You can't just *know* about the power in the blood of Jesus; you have to *declare* it with the words of your mouth. Matthew 12:37 AMP says, **For by your words you will be justified and acquitted, and by your words you will be condemned and sentenced.** When you plead the blood of Jesus, you are acquitted instead of condemned. But if you start saying the things the devil wants you to say, you sentence yourself to defeat by your own words.

So we see that "pleading the blood" is a powerful phrase that lines up with Scripture. It is *not* just an empty religious term or an old Pentecostal term.

Actually, the Pentecostals of old knew some truths about the blood of Jesus that the modern Church has let go of. But in the last few years, Christians have begun to regain what the devil had stolen away from the Body of Christ about the blood of Jesus.

Personally, I'm believing we won't stop learning until we're walking in the fullness of divine protection and deliverance by the power of the blood.

Putting Into Place Our Protection

So as the children of Israel applied the blood of the lamb over their doors, we are to plead the blood of Jesus over our lives—including our children. That's the way we put into place the protection God has set aside for us.

For instance, when I enter an airplane, I lay my hand on the door and say, "I plead the blood of Jesus. I apply the blood of Jesus to the doorpost of this airplane. This plane is going to get me where I'm going. My belongings will arrive safely, and the trip will be smooth and without incident." I don't say those words loudly, but I do say them out loud. I don't act strangely or draw attention to myself. But I also don't leave anything out.

My belongings get to my destination better when I plead the blood of Jesus over them. My airplanes arrive where they are supposed to arrive. And as I leave the airplane, I thank the Lord for getting me to my destination safely.

I'm not afraid to get on an airplane, but at the same time, I will not miss the chance to take advantage of what the Lord has given me. I am going to close and lock every

door to the enemy. And I don't care
devil has an assignment against on t
take *me* down.

I also plead the blood of Jesus every time my fam.,
in the car to go somewhere. And I make sure my teenage
daughters, who are driving now, do the same thing whenever
they get behind the wheel.

I want my family protected. In fact, I have made covenant
with the Lord and with my family that we are not going to be
taken out of this world through tragedy, accidents or any
other strategy of the devil. We are not going to let the enemy
have control over us. We are going to go together in the
Rapture. Or if the Lord tarries, we will all live to an old age.
We won't go home to heaven until we are satisfied that we
have completed what God has called us to do on this earth.

That's what you need to do as well with *your* family. Settle
it in your heart before heaven and earth that the devil isn't
going to take out any member of your family through his
strategies. Don't wait until your child is in a coma or until
you're standing in a bank during a robbery. Make that
covenant with the Lord right now.

That decision will give you the determination to hold fast
to the Word when a storm comes. It will also keep you from
listening to the devil when he tries to convince you, "This
tragedy is God's will for you."

No, it *isn't* God's will. God's will is not that you or your children suffer harm or perish, but that you live a long life. He needs all of us to help fulfill His purposes on this earth.

It seems so absurd when you think about it. Why would God try to kill you and your family members if He needs every one of you? A landowner doesn't send all the field hands back to the main house for a rest at peak harvest time.

God's Way to Escape Judgment

When you continually apply the blood of Jesus to the doorposts of your life by faith, you can live in complete confidence that the devil can't touch your family because God has them in His hands.

But why is this so? Why *can't* the devil gain access to your family when you plead the blood of Jesus over them every day? To find the answer to that question, we have to understand the way God provided for us to escape judgment. Let's go back to Exodus 12:12:

> **For I will pass through the land of Egypt this night, and will smite all the firstborn in the land of Egypt, both man and beast; and against all the gods of Egypt *I will execute judgment:* I am the Lord.**

When the death angel passed through Egypt, the only reason the angel was able to kill every firstborn was that the Egyptians lacked any divine protection. When God said, "I will execute judgment," He didn't mean He was going to send out the death angel just to see how many people He could kill. He simply meant that death would pass through the land, and because the Egyptians were not protected behind the blood, they would be subject to judgment.

But in the land of Goshen, God had given the Israelites a way out. In verse 13, He said, **And the blood shall be to you for a token upon the houses where ye are: and when I see the blood, I will pass over you.** The Israelites had the choice to either accept or reject God's way. Those who obeyed God's command to apply the blood of a lamb to their doors were protected behind the blood and they escaped judgment when death passed through.

Well, nothing has changed since then. When the blood is present, death still cannot come in. However, today we no longer apply the blood of a literal lamb to our literal doorposts. Now we have the blood of Jesus to protect us. He shed His blood once and for all to purchase our complete deliverance from every work of the enemy.

Notice that God said, **The blood shall be to you for a token upon the houses where ye are.** The blood of the lamb was a *token*, or a *showing*, of God's power. The devil saw that token and he couldn't prevail against it.

But today we don't have just a token; we have the real thing. How much more does the devil see the blood of Jesus covering our families and know that he cannot prevail against us?

Poor Children in a Rich Father's House

Sadly, many Christians choose to live their lives without applying the blood of Jesus to the doorposts of their lives. Failing to actively believe God for protection, they leave themselves vulnerable to the devil's attacks.

But we can't afford to be passive about protection. We're living in a horrible day. In the words of Charles Dickens, it is both the best of times and the worst of times.

For those in the world, it is a dangerous time without hope. Disasters and tragedies abound, and the chances are good that, at some point in their lives, they will be caught in one of them. Maybe they will become a victim of crime, of a car accident or of an earthquake that kills thousands. Regardless of the circumstances in which these people find themselves caught, one thing is sure—without the blood of Jesus, they have no supernatural recourse nor hope of deliverance.

Christians are not in that same plight. They do have a way of escape; however, too often they are ignorant of that fact. They don't know they can live each day with a shield of divine protection around them. They don't know that they don't have to be pushed to and fro with the world according to the devil's whims. Therefore, they go their entire lives receiving only one benefit of Jesus' blood—that is, the right to go to heaven when they die. They never know what it is to live a separate life, protected from all harm by the blood of Jesus.

What a shame that is. It's like being a member of a rich family, yet living like a poor man all your life. You never have anything good to eat. You don't have decent clothes to wear or a decent home to live in. But you know that when you die, they will build a beautiful golden crypt to lay your body in.

That's the way God sees it when His people don't appropriate the divine protection He has provided. It's just like any other promise in the Word. If Christians don't believe God for protection, they aren't going to enjoy the benefits of that particular promise. The blessing of supernatural protection will go unclaimed and unused unless they learn how to receive it from their Heavenly Father.

Strangers from the Covenant

Some Christians even pray, "If I die before I wake, I pray the Lord my soul to take." Not only are these people unsure whether or not they will die before they wake up, but they aren't even sure the Lord will take their soul if they do.

Doubting God's ability to protect His children is an example of religious thinking, which the enemy uses to keep Christians defeated and under his thumb.

Because of religious traditions, people have not received the blood of Jesus as a true and practical help in their everyday life.

> **For [although] they hold a form of piety (true religion), they deny and reject and are strangers to the power of it....**
>
> **2 Timothy 3:5 AMP**

According to Ephesians 2:12,13,19, we have been brought near to God and His promises by the blood.

> **That at that time ye were without Christ, being aliens from the commonwealth of Israel, and strangers from the covenants of promise, having no hope, and without God in the world: But now in Christ Jesus ye who sometimes were far off are made nigh by the blood of Christ...Now therefore ye are no more strangers and foreigners, but fellow citizens with the saints, and of the household of God.**

We are no longer strangers to the covenants of promise. What a shame to live as though we were! Without realizing it, we have often doubted the power of and thereby spurned the blood of Jesus by not putting it into action in our lives and in the lives of our children. For instance, whenever we are afraid of something the enemy is trying to do to our families, we have just discounted the blood of Jesus as our answer. In essence, we are saying, "Well, the blood can't do the job here. This is just too big for God." We have denied the power of the blood of Jesus and settled for religion, and in doing so, we have failed to honor the blood of Jesus.

When people receive salvation but don't experience any life change, healing or prosperity as a result of that salvation, they have spurned the blood and many other precious promises because religion—traditions of men—have caused them to be strangers from the covenants of promise. The same is true of church denominations that have taken songs about the blood out of their hymnals, claiming that such songs "scare" the children.

The blood of Jesus is the very key to our existence. *It is our very life.* We as believers must honor the blood above sin, sickness, problems or lack. After all, isn't that exactly what the Father did? He honored Jesus' blood over our sin. He declared us free from sickness because of the blood shed on our behalf. We must lay hold of this and receive it as more than just a church tradition or a Bible story.

The Church cannot survive in power without a real revelation of the blood of Jesus. The devil knows this, so one of his main tricks is to keep Christians from knowing about the sure protection that is available to them through the blood.

Even many Word-believing, Spirit-filled Christians haven't been able to firmly lay hold of their deliverance because they haven't understood the power in the blood of Jesus. Therefore, they doubt God's ability to protect them and their families from *all* harm.

Praise God, doubt is erased as we begin to receive the benefits purchased for us through the precious blood of Jesus. We will never again be as strangers and outsiders, living as though we had no covenant with God. How that grieves the Holy Spirit!

The Holy Spirit is the Minister of grace; it is His delight to deliver us through the saving power of the blood. Therefore, it grieves Him when He is restrained by our disobedience from imparting the grace to protect, heal and prosper us. He isn't grieved for Jesus' sake, but for *our* sake. He is limited in ministering His blessings to us unless we honor, highly prize and *appropriate* the blood of Jesus in our lives.

Understanding the Nature of Judgment

We saw in Exodus 12:12 that God said He would *execute judgment*. To understand what He meant by that, you must first understand the true nature of judgment.

First, it's important to understand that God didn't invent sin. Everything God created was good. It was the devil who introduced sin, and he has been twisting God's perfect creation ever since.

Second, judgment is not God beating people over the head because they have sinned. God doesn't say, "Well, he did this wrong, so I'm going to give him cancer or AIDS to teach him a lesson."

God already decreed that **the wages of sin is death** (Romans 6:23). He was saying that death is what sin leads to, and death is the price that must be paid.

That one verse alone tells us what we need to know about the nature of judgment. It tells us that if we practice sin, we open the door to the enemy's works of death and destruction.

After God decreed that the wages of sin is death, there was no getting around that judgment because He spoke the truth. He laid out that eternal principle for us once, and He never has to do it again. Psalm 111:7-8 AMP confirms this:

> **The works of His hands are [absolute] truth and justice [faithful and right]; and all His decrees and precepts are sure (fixed, established, and trustworthy). They stand fast and are established forever and ever and are done in [absolute] truth and uprightness.**

All of God's decrees are fixed. That's the way it is. Those divine decrees aren't going to change. And anything that goes against them will reap the reward of judgment.

God isn't out there saying, "I'm going to do this to judge that sin, and I'll do that to judge this other sin." He doesn't have to judge every situation. He doesn't see a sinner today and say, "You're living a homosexual lifestyle, so I am going to strike you with AIDS." He has already decreed that sin leads to death. That's the way it is, and it is not going to change.

Think for a moment about the way lawyers argue their case before a judge in a court of law. Lawyers often refer to a list of cases that support the way they want the judgment to go. They do that to demonstrate that in similar cases, other judges have already made a decision. The lawyers hope that the current judge will agree with those past decisions and rule in their favor.

A well-known example of a settled judgment is Roe vs. Wade. Without a move of God that Supreme Court judgment supporting abortion is going to stand up in court. There is no need for a lawyer in a lower court to argue the issue again. Why is this? Because *the judgment has already been made.* Until a new law is passed, abortion will be legal even if not moral.

That's also the way judgment works as far as God is concerned. He already determined that the wages of sin is death. Therefore, as sin runs rampant on the earth, judgment occurs because of that previously established spiritual law.

That's why God told the children of Israel, "If you will do what I tell you to do, you will be blessed. If you don't, you will be cursed." (See Deuteronomy 28.)

God didn't create those curses; He didn't create the repercussions of sin. Sin caused the curse. God just tells us how to avoid sin's results. He lets us know that sin is a path that inevitably leads to death and destruction.

So when you think about all the bad things that happen in this earth, realize that those calamities are just the natural destination to which sin leads. There is no way to get away from that fact apart from the saving power of Jesus. You have to get on a different road and start heading a different direction in order to arrive at a different destination.

My father, Kenneth Copeland, gave a wonderful illustration of this that I can't improve upon. Suppose you are driving down a highway and you read a sign that says, "Austin, 200 miles." If you don't want to go to the city of Austin, you better make a U-turn—because if you stay on that road, you're going to end up in Austin!

In the same way, God puts up signposts to let you know which way you're headed spiritually. If you stay on the road to sin, or if you don't actively do something to get off that road, you're going to end up in judgment. So if you don't want to end up there, you had better turn around.

God graciously gave everyone who has ever lived on this earth a way to escape judgment through the death and resurrection of His Son, Jesus Christ. Even before Jesus came, God gave people a temporary way of escape through the sacrificial blood of animals. Having decreed that the wages of sin is death, God has *never* failed to provide man with a way of escape.

So how do you get off the road to judgment? And how do you make sure your children stay off that road so they can reach God's destination of deliverance and victory? You do it by obeying the fixed decree that God instituted on the night of the Passover: When the blood is present, death cannot come in. You apply the blood of Jesus to the doorposts of your life, and you never stop speaking the protection of the blood for you and your family by faith!

God Isn't the Source of Calamity

A lot of Christians tell people that tragedy is God judging their sins. But that isn't true. Tragedy and trouble are not from God. *Good* is from God, and bad is from the devil. It's just that simple. Actually, it's too simple to mess up, but we find a way to do it anyway!

God has been so maligned in these last days. His Name has been so dishonored with false accusations. People say all the time, "Well, God caused that disaster" or "God allowed that tragedy to happen." These people think God is behind the horrible things they hear about on the news, whether it is school shootings, fatal accidents or natural disasters.

But God is *not* the one causing those tragic events. The terrible things that happen in the world are not "acts of God," nor are they God's way of punishing people or bringing them to a low point where they will finally repent. That isn't what judgment is.

Actually, people who think God causes bad things to happen by His sovereign will are not thinking that premise all the way through. Otherwise, they would see that it just doesn't make sense.

Tragedy is not God's will. We know that because we have a copy of God's will—the written Word of God—and it says, **Every *good* gift and every *perfect* gift is from above, and cometh down from the Father of lights, with whom is no variableness, neither shadow of turning** (James 1:17). Our Heavenly Father gives only good and perfect gifts. Tragedy is a part of the *devil's* bag of tricks—a part of the judgment to which sin inevitably leads.

Actually, the simplest way to define judgment is this: *As the earth fills up with sin, the overflow is judgment.*

The world has been on the fast track to judgment for a number of years now. Just watch the evening news, and you'll see what I mean! When you can watch a doctor kill someone on a television news documentary and it is deemed acceptable, or when millions of unborn babies can be killed and it doesn't bother too many people—you know that the earth is filling up with sin!

This earth is groaning and shaking under the burden of mankind's sin. And when that sin overflows, the end result is an increase in judgment.

Just as judgment went through the land of Egypt on the night of the Passover feast, today judgment is sweeping through the earth in unprecedented measures. We are witnessing more calamities and large-scale natural disasters around the world than ever before. As an example, just consider the recent earthquake in India that killed more than twenty thousand people!

Governments might try to make things better through programs and policies. However, there is ultimately nothing man can do to stem the tide of judgment on the earth.

But *God* has already done something! He sent His Son, Jesus, to give all people a way out, and He is doing everything He possibly can to change people's hearts and help them start living for Him so they can get off the road to judgment.

The truth is, although the earth is filling up with sin in this hour, it is also filling up with God's glory at the same time. And as Romans 5:20 says, where sin abounds, grace does much more abound!

That divine grace will protect you and your children, even if you find yourselves in the place where judgment is occurring. You may ask, "But how could God deliver us in the middle of an earthquake that kills thirty thousand people?" Well, Psalm 91:7 says, **A thousand shall fall at thy side, and ten thousand at thy right hand; but it shall not come nigh thee.** God says He can and will protect you, even when death and destruction are all around you. The promise is there if you want to claim it and are willing to apply the blood of Jesus to the doorposts of your life.

The Case of God's Sovereignty

The lie that God is behind both the man-made and the natural disasters that happen in this world is just a trick of the devil to keep us from trusting God and appropriating His promise of protection in our lives. If we believe that lie, we conclude, "Well, God is sovereign, so I have no control over what might happen to my family and me in the future."

Many Christians have that attitude. They say, "Since God is sovereign, whatever happens to us is His will. We just have to bear it because it's all part of His plan."

But that is a very deadly thought process that will keep believers from being able to move into what God wants them to do. For instance, suppose these Christians were in a situation where a terrorist was pointing a gun at them and they sensed the Holy Spirit prompting them to walk over to the criminal and boldly share the gospel with him. Without a solid assurance that God will protect them, how would they be able to do that? That example may seem dramatic.

But if they believe that whatever happens, good or bad, is God's will, how can they have any confidence that God will protect their children from all harm? Yes, God is sovereign. But God sovereignly gave us dominion over the enemy through the Name of Jesus, the blood of Jesus and the anointed Word. God sovereignly gave us covenant promises. And He sovereignly decided to give us the choice whether or not to appropriate those promises in our lives.

God will not take back that choice. He isn't going to change. Everything would cease to exist if He turned back on His Word and did something differently than what He has already said, because what He has said is the truth.

When tragedy hits, Christians who argue the sovereignty of God say, "Well, it must have been God's will, or this terrible tragedy wouldn't have happened to me." That is such a spiritually lazy way to look at life. These people are actually saying, "I have no part to play in what happens to me."

No, that's wrong! God's Word says we are to be alert and vigilant against the devil's attacks. We can't just go around thinking, "I'm a Christian, so God is going to protect me" and then assume that God will prevent anything bad from happening to us.

Protection is not automatic. In fact, I haven't found anything in God's Word that is automatic! Even salvation must be believed, asked for and received.

For some reason, we seem to think that God's promises are going to be fulfilled for us just because we're Christians. But it just doesn't work that way. Someone once said to me, "But I thought that when you got saved you were automatically protected." The Spirit of God spoke up inside me and I told her, "Well, that would be true if the enemy wasn't trying every day to..." And she finished my sentence for me, "...to take it away from you!" I saw the light come on in her eyes. God has placed the responsibility in *our* laps to find out what He has to say and then appropriate it in our lives.

If we don't fulfill that God-ordained responsibility, we'll go along with the world's flow until we end up in judgment just like everyone else. Sure, we'll get to heaven (possibly sooner than planned), but we could have gotten there a lot easier and a lot more protected.

I'll give you an example of another dangerous way that Christians often think. A couple who has just suffered the loss of their baby might go to a pastor for counsel and hear these "comforting" words: "Well, God must have needed a flower for His garden. He needed your little baby to come home to Him."

What an insult to God! What a trampling of the blood of Jesus to say that something the enemy has done is the work of God!

Be very careful not to say such words yourself. If you do, it will hinder your ability to receive the promises of God in your own life. It's just better to say, "I don't know how I let this happen, but I'm going to search the Word and see what God says about it."

God *will* answer your questions, but not when you come to Him accusingly and ask, "Lord, why did You do this?" Anger toward God is always defeating. The devil will use it to take you further from the answer, and further from God.

God once said something arresting to me on my way to teach high-school students about the divine protection afforded us by the blood of Jesus. I'll never forget the pain in His voice as He said, *I have a hard time convincing My children to trust Me fully with their lives because they still don't firmly believe that I'll deliver and protect them.*

I understood what the Lord was trying to get across to me. After all, it's very difficult to have courage in what you do for the Lord if you're not assured of His protection. If you think God allows tragedies to occur in your life just to teach you something, you are going to find it difficult to entrust your life or your children to Him.

God was saying, "My people won't give their lives fully to Me because they don't trust Me. How *can* they trust Me if they think I might decide that allowing their child to be martyred is the best way to further the gospel?"

God knows what it is like to be a parent. He is the Father! He knows what it is to see your son die. But, praise the

Lord—because He knew that pain, we don't have to! He is offering us assurance that our children will be protected. And He says we can have that strong assurance! All we have to do is walk in the light of the Word and appropriate His promise of protection.

Just imagine Jesus walking on this earth today. If someone held a gun to His face, would He be afraid that He might get shot? Absolutely not. Jesus would know beyond a shadow of a doubt that His Father would deliver Him.

Well, God will deliver our children as well. We just need to get off the road to judgment the world is on and start going the other way, protecting our children by the precious blood of Jesus!

CHAPTER 3

Protection Through God's Grace

O ne of the most important things I've learned
about the blood of Jesus is this: *When we plead the
blood of Jesus over our children, we make allowances for their mistakes, as well as our own mistakes and shortcomings.* Now, don't
get religious on me—let me explain.

That doesn't mean we can live any way we want to live.
But it does mean God has made a way out of the place of
judgment for us. Through the blood of Jesus, He has set us
free from the guilt of sin! First John 1:7 says it very plainly:
**But if we walk in the light as He is in the light, we have fel-
lowship one with another, and the blood of Jesus Christ
his Son cleanseth us from all unrighteousness.**

No Weapon Shall Prosper Because of the Blood

I want you to look at Isaiah 54:17, one of my favorite Scriptures. It's a part of a very powerful chapter that's just full of promises you can stake your life on.

The Lord recently opened up this verse to me to help me understand how divine protection is available by the blood of Jesus through the avenue of His grace.

> **No weapon that is formed against thee shall prosper; and every tongue that shall rise against thee in judgment thou shalt condemn. This is the heritage of the servants of the Lord, and their righteousness is of me, saith the Lord.**

The Lord brought this Scripture to my mind a while back when we came upon an accident on the way to take the kids to Superkid Academy Camp. A mother had made the mistake of having more kids in her van than she had seatbelts. She also let her 16-year-old son drive the overloaded van on the country roads. As her son drove around a corner a little too fast, the van went off the road and rolled several times, totaling the vehicle.

Not far behind this van full of kids, I was also driving to the Superkid Academy Camp with my children and two other junior counselors. Shortly after the van went off the road, we came upon the detour that had been set up because of the accident. I thought, *I better turn around and see if that accident involved any of our campers.*

Sure enough, it did. The emergency personnel were already there, checking all the occupants of the van for injuries. I drove up and talked to one of the emergency workers on the scene. He told me, "I can't believe no one was hurt in this accident. They should have *all* been hurt!"

What was the devil trying to do? He was trying to ruin Superkid Academy Camp for the summer. He was trying to ruin the lives of the four families represented in the van. He was trying to take out some powerful, on-fire Christian kids who know how to pray and believe the Word. And he was trying to ruin the lives of that mother and her son. Just think what it would have been like for them if any lives had been lost while that young man had been driving!

The devil was trying to steal, kill and destroy everything he could in this situation. He was trying to take out anyone he could take out. *Nevertheless, the enemy wasn't able to do what he wanted to do.*

The van was lying in a big field next to the road and looked just awful. But not one of the children had been hurt in the accident. Even the children who hadn't been wearing seatbelts escaped without a scratch! The only person injured at all was the mother, who sustained a few cuts on her arm.

We piled everyone into the other cars that had stopped in the meantime and were also headed to the camp. The young man who had been driving the van rode in my car. On our way to the camp, the Lord really put it on my heart to start ministering to this young man because he was feeling very guilty.

I said to him, "Let me ask you something. Did you plead the blood of Jesus this morning?"

"Well, yes," he replied. "We plead the blood of Jesus whenever we go anywhere. This morning we also prayed and took Communion before we left."

The young man continued, "I knew I shouldn't have been driving. I had thoughts that something might happen."

I said, "Well, it *is* important to listen to your spirit."

Right then the Lord reminded me of Isaiah 54:17, and I realized why the Lord had supernaturally protected everyone involved in the accident, even though mistakes were made.

This verse says, **No weapon that is formed against thee shall prosper.** It also says that **every tongue that shall rise against thee in judgment thou shalt condemn.** In this case, it was the devil's wagging tongue that rose up in judgment against the mother and son and said, "You messed up, so I'm going to kill someone today. I'm going to ruin someone's life today."

The devil isn't just trying to be an inconvenience in his strategies against you or your children. His goal is to *kill and destroy.* In every way he can, he's trying to get rid of you.

But the devil can't do that if you don't allow him to! God promises in this verse that no weapon formed against you will succeed in its evil intent. Then He says, **This is the heritage of the servants of the Lord, and their righteousness is of me, saith the Lord.**

Walking in Jesus' Footsteps

The Lord was giving me all these insights so I could share them with this young man as we were driving along to camp. Then I began saying something I had never thought of before.

I told the teenager, "You weren't walking in your own righteousness today, so don't let the devil lie to you and convince you that you're guilty. You pled the blood of Jesus. And even though you messed up—even though you shouldn't have driven with more kids in the car than you had seatbelts—this is what the Lord told me: *When you plead the blood of Jesus, you put yourself in His footsteps.* You purposefully live your life in His righteousness, and the devil can't fight that.

"Now, as a child," I continued, "it is important that you obey your parents. And when God prompts you to do something, it is important to listen to your spirit. It is also important to obey the laws of the land. But when we plead the blood of Jesus, we make allowances for our own mistakes and shortcomings, for the times we don't pick up on what the Holy Spirit is saying to us."

It's always easier to do something the right way. There is almost certainly going to be an irritating price to pay when you're disobedient or when you don't listen to the Spirit of God.

For instance, that mother's van was totaled. She also had to go to the doctor's office so the cuts on her arm could be stitched up. Those consequences for her mistake were definitely annoying, but they were not life threatening.

That is the effect of divine protection. When you plead the blood of Jesus by faith, God will deliver you to the other side without loss of life—whether it is your life, your children's lives or your spouse's life. You may endure inconvenient consequences for not listening to God, but you will not suffer irreversible tragedy.

On the other hand, you can't just go along sinning on purpose, living your life any old way you want to, and then say, "Well, I'll just plead the blood, and everything will be okay."

In the case of the van accident, that mother and son didn't set out on that trip trying to see how far they could get with God. They weren't trying to blatantly go against the Lord's instructions. Their hearts were right; they just missed it.

Psalm 24:3-4 says that we have to come to God *with clean hands and pure hearts.* We can't live a sinful life and then expect everything to go along right for us.

But although it's true that we have to maintain a pure heart, it is also true that we all mess up sometimes. In light of that fact, isn't it good to know that God doesn't require 100-percent perfection at this stage of the game? Instead, He has made it possible for us to walk in the footsteps of Jesus, in His 100-percent perfection, clothed in *His* righteousness and not our own.

We have a goal we're headed toward. We are learning to listen to our spirits and to hear the voice of the Holy Spirit. We are endeavoring to do the right thing in every situation. And we purpose to plead the blood of Jesus over our families every day. As we do these things, the devil won't be able to touch our children or us.

But if we mess up during this learning process, we can be confident of this as long as we keep our families under the protection of the blood: Our mistake may cost us some time and money, but it won't cost us our lives or the lives of our children. If we will faithfully plead the blood of Jesus, God will deliver our families with our lives intact. That's a promise we can claim!

So if you do something wrong or miss the Spirit of God's leading, just repent and then say, "I plead *not guilty,* because I plead the blood of Jesus!" Your faith in the blood puts you in Jesus' footsteps and provides you and your children with divine protection—all because of *God's grace.*

What Is Grace?

I've heard many definitions for grace. By one definition, grace is unmerited favor; by another, it is God's ability to do things you can't do. But the best definition I've ever heard is this: *Grace is God looking at you the same way He looks at His Son.* It is God judging you as though you were Jesus.

What does that mean for you? Well, can you imagine the Heavenly Father looking at Jesus and saying, "I'm not going to do that for You"? Absolutely not!

Jesus died in your place and shed His blood so you could stand in His righteousness. As you plead the blood of Jesus over your family, God sees you and your loved ones the same way He sees Jesus—deserving of the same blessings and the same angelic protection He afforded His Son when He walked this earth.

How does God see Jesus? Well, He sees a Son who doesn't make mistakes. God judges Jesus as free from sickness, sin, calamity and spiritual death. The good news is that Jesus paid the price for you so that you could be free as well!

When you appropriate the blood of Jesus in your life, God has to look at you and say, "You're free, you're clean, and you're in My righteousness. You are covered by My wings."

Now, the devil would love to lie to you and say, "God can't deliver you from this mess because you brought it on yourself."

But as you and your family stand in Jesus' footsteps, it doesn't matter if you've made mistakes. It doesn't matter if your children mess up. It doesn't matter if you're guilty or innocent because God's deliverance isn't based on you; it's based on Jesus. You can plead the blood of Jesus, and His grace covers your mistakes as you live in His righteousness.

For example, you may ask, "Yes, but what if my mistake involves a lot of charge card debt?"

The devil has kept so many believers bowed down with guilt and discouragement because of this particular problem. The enemy whispers to their minds, *God can't deliver you from charge card debt because you used your card to charge an entire closet full of clothes with it! That was selfish. You knew better than to do that. God can't deliver you because you put yourself in that situation.*

But God judges us according to the way He sees Jesus, and Jesus doesn't have charge card problems. That means we are judged as free from charge card problems too.

We can come before God and say, "Lord, I repent. Please deliver me from debt. I plead the blood of Jesus over my finances." God then judges us with the same favor He gives Jesus and responds, "You are perfect in My eyes. Therefore, I gladly deliver you from debt!" That is a manifestation of God's grace!

Here's another example: The devil accuses a person in his mind, saying, *God can't heal you from cancer because you smoked. You knew it was bad for you, but you did it anyway for years and years and years.*

But Jesus doesn't have a problem with smoking. God doesn't look at Jesus and say, "Well, I can't heal You of lung cancer because You used to smoke."

So God looks at that believer and makes a judgment based on how He judges Jesus. Even if that person smoked for most of his life, he can still trust in God's measureless grace and therefore stand confidently on God's promise to heal his body.

In the same way, God protects us as though we were Jesus when we walk in His righteousness. And the Word says that Jesus could have called 10,000 angels. If He could, we can!

The Source of God's Grace

Why is this true? Romans 5:21 gives us the answer. It says that *grace reigns through righteousness.* Jesus' righteousness is the doorway through which God's grace enters our lives.

God can provide grace to us because we are made righteous through the blood of Jesus. He now sees us the way He sees Jesus. His grace on our lives isn't based on our good works or our perfection; it's based on *Jesus'* perfection. As Isaiah 54:17 says, **Their righteousness is of me, saith the Lord.**

That's why no weapon formed against you or your children can prosper. When you plead the blood of Jesus over your family, you are living fully in the righteousness of Jesus. You and your children are literally standing before the Father in the footsteps of Jesus. You can therefore say, "It doesn't matter what I or my children did wrong. It doesn't matter if we are guilty or not guilty. I plead the blood!" I receive the righteousness of Jesus.

Too many Christians are trying to base their protection on their own ability. They have forgotten their covenant of divine protection. They might say a little prayer and read a Scripture or two in the morning. But then they go on, trying to get through the day on their own.

But when you plead the blood of Jesus over yourself and your children each morning, it does something to you. It sets your mind and your spirit right to realize at the beginning of each day, *My family is getting through this day protected by the grace of God and the blood of Jesus.*

Draw Near for Righteous Judgments

Isaiah 58:2 AMP talks about the children of Israel coming to God for righteous judgments.

> **Yet they** [God's people] **seek, inquire for, and require Me daily and delight** [externally] **to know My ways, as [if they were in reality] a nation that did righteousness and forsook not the ordinance of their God. They ask of Me righteous judgments, they delight to draw near to God [in visible ways].**

Now, in context, God is actually getting after His people, telling them that their spiritual actions need to be a reflection of an inward change of heart. But I want us to look at how He describes those actions: **They ask of Me righteous judgments, they delight to draw near to God.**

That's similar to the New Covenant admonition to **draw near to the throne of grace** (Hebrews 4:16 AMP). You have already been given a righteous judgment. God has made you the righteousness of God in Christ. (2 Corinthians 5:21.) He has given you promises that have already been bought and paid for by the blood of His Son. Those promises belong to you and your family. Now you just have to lay hold of them, standing on His righteous judgments by faith in the blood of Jesus.

As you plead the blood of Jesus, you are coming boldly before God's throne according to His righteous judgment to receive His mercy and grace for your family. You are saying, "We're not in ourselves perfect, Lord, but I plead the blood of Jesus over our lives so we can walk in *His* footsteps. I want my family to live in His righteousness today." When you do that, God is always faithful to give you His grace!

When you enter the throne room based on the blood of Jesus, you are coming to the Father asking Him to judge you with the same "measuring stick" He judges Jesus. And when He does what you ask, the miracle of grace is that you actually measure up!

You don't have to live according to the way of the world. You don't have to live subjected to the tricks of the enemy or to the misguided people who follow him. You and your children can live every day in the footsteps of Jesus!

For instance, suppose Jesus lived in the flesh on this earth today, and He was standing in a bank when thieves burst in to rob it. There is no way those thieves would be able to hurt Jesus. He would be able to turn that entire situation around!

Well, that's who *you* are. You have Jesus Christ on the inside of you. And when you plead the blood of Jesus, you make yourself more aware of who you are in Him.

As you faithfully plead the blood of Jesus over yourself and your children, it doesn't change only the circumstances that surround you. It changes *you*. It changes the way you react in difficult situations.

It is easier to respond with confidence and faith when you know you're standing in Jesus' footsteps. No matter what the circumstances, you can rest in the knowledge that your family is protected from harm by the precious blood of Jesus—because grace reigns through righteousness, and you are righteous in Christ!

CHAPTER 4

Our Sanctuary—
the Holy of Holies

I want to take you to some key Scriptures to show you two basic principles for protecting your children. First, *your deliverance from evil, tragedy, sickness or sudden death is by faith in the blood of Jesus.* Second, *your faith in the blood is executed and entered into by the words of your mouth.*

I also want to show you *why* these two principles are true. It all has to do with *entering the Holy of Holies*—the eternal sanctuary of God's presence.

The Way Into God's Presence—by Blood

Let's start by going back to the Old Testament and see how God made a way for His people to enter His presence by means of sacrificial blood:

The Lord said to Moses, Tell Aaron your brother he must not come at all times into the Holy of Holies within the veil before the mercy seat upon the ark, lest he die; for I will appear in the cloud on the mercy seat.

Leviticus 16:2

Moses' brother, Aaron, was the high priest, but he couldn't just go into the Holy of Holies anytime or any way he wanted to. He could only go in once a year at the appointed time, and he had to do everything just as God had instructed.

The high priest couldn't forget the smallest detail. Every "t" had to be crossed and every "i" dotted. He had to wash the right way. He had to say the right things. He had to sprinkle the blood of the right kind of animals. He had to follow God's instructions exactly to the letter. If the high priest's sin wasn't covered when he went into the presence of God, he wouldn't come out alive!

That didn't mean God was trying to make it hard for His people to come to Him. He wasn't trying to separate Himself from man because He was prideful. God was actually *protecting* man. He knew that sin could not exist in His presence.

Darkness cannot live in the light. The smallest bit of light can dispel darkness, but darkness cannot overcome the light.

That's why God couldn't gather Adam and Eve in His arms to comfort them after they had sinned. That would be the natural instinct of any loving father. But if God had done that, He would have killed them with His goodness because sin is destroyed in the presence of His glory.

So God in His mercy made a way for fallen man to draw near to Him, instituting the slaying of an innocent animal as a temporary remedy for sin. In Leviticus 16, He gave detailed instructions to the high priest, the people's representative, on how to enter into His presence. It had to be by blood, and it had to be just right. (Just read the rest of Leviticus 16, and you'll see what I mean!)

In fact, Jewish oral tradition tells us the other priests would tie a rope around the high priest. After he entered the Holy of Holies, they would listen for the jingling of the bells sewn to the bottom of the high priest's robe. (Exodus 39:25.) If those bells had ever quit jingling, it would have meant he hadn't prepared himself correctly and it was time to pull out his lifeless body!

The high priest would take the blood of that sacrifice and enter God's presence for one purpose: to obtain a good judgment for himself and for the people. If the priest did everything correctly, they would be judged free from sin for one year.

Draw Near by the Blood

Interestingly, the Hebrew word for "sacrifice" is from the same root as "to come near, to approach, to become closely involved in a relationship with someone."[1] The blood of the sacrificial animal enabled the high priest to enter the Holy of Holies and draw near to the mercy seat of God. If he hadn't brought the blood of that sacrifice, the sin in his life would have killed him before he ever reached the mercy seat.

It wasn't that God needed a gift from the people or wanted them to do something for Him. Man needed the blood to atone for his sin so he could draw near to God.

Well, today we have the blood of Jesus, Who was the perfect Sacrifice. His precious blood takes care of our sin once and for all, allowing us to draw near to the throne of God to receive mercy and grace for every situation.

Hebrews 9:12-14 AMP tells us the magnitude of what Jesus did for us through His death and resurrection:

> **He went once for all into the [Holy of] Holies [of heaven], not by virtue of the blood of goats and calves [by which to make reconciliation between God and man], but His own**

---

[1] The Holy Temple of Jerusalem, Chaim Richman, The Temple Institute and Carta, Jerusalem, 1977 Carta, The Israel Map and Publishing Company, Ltd.

blood, having found and secured a complete redemption (an everlasting release for us).

For if [the mere] sprinkling of unholy and defiled persons with blood of goats and bulls and with the ashes of a burnt heifer is sufficient for the purification of the body, how much more surely shall the blood of Christ, Who by virtue of [His] eternal Spirit [His own preexistent divine personality] has offered Himself as an unblemished sacrifice to God, purify our consciences from dead works and lifeless observances to serve the [ever] living God?

God is saying here, "If a goat, a bull or a heifer could provide a temporary redemption for sin under the Old Covenant, how much more will the blood of Jesus Christ provide an eternal and absolutely complete redemption for you under the New Covenant?"

Let's go on to verses 18-20 AMP:

So even the [old] first covenant (God's will) was not inaugurated and ratified and put in force without the shedding of blood.

For when every command of the Law had been read out by Moses to all the people, he took the blood of slain calves and goats, together

**with water and scarlet wool and a bunch of
hyssop, and sprinkled both the Book (the roll
of the Law and covenant) itself and all the
people, saying these words:** *This is the blood
that seals and ratifies the agreement* **(the testament, the covenant) which God commanded
[me to deliver to] you.**

Under the Old Covenant, Moses used a bunch of hyssop
(which symbolizes our faith) to sprinkle the blood of the
animal sacrifice over the people as atonement for their sins.
Then he declared, "This is the blood that seals and ratifies
our covenant with God!"

Notice that Moses spoke those words with his mouth.
This was an Old Testament demonstration of the important
principle I mentioned earlier: *Your faith in the blood is executed
and entered into by the words of your mouth.*

Instead of hyssop, you use faith to apply the blood of
Jesus to your life. But as you plead the blood of Jesus over
yourself and your children by faith, you are actually saying
the same thing Moses did: "This is the blood that seals and
ratifies the covenant I have with You, Lord. And part of that
covenant is Your promise to protect us!"

Verse 22 AMP tells us why our approach to God must be
by means of sacrificial blood:

[In fact] under the Law almost everything is purified by means of blood, and without the shedding of blood there is neither release from sin and its guilt nor the remissions of the due and merited punishment for sins.

Aaron went into the Holy of Holies by the blood of an animal. But Jesus took His very own blood into God's presence. In doing so, Jesus made the way, tearing down the veil that had always separated man from the presence of God.

Jesus, the "Lamb for our house," paid the price to enter into the Holy of Holies by the power of His blood. All that is left for us to do is to apply the blood He shed for us to our lives—to declare by faith, "This is the blood that seals my covenant with God!"

As we do that, we are purified and set free not only from sin, but also from all things pertaining to death and judgment—the due and merited punishment for our sin. We can now enter the Holy of Holies for ourselves by the power in the blood of Jesus according to Hebrews 10:19-20 AMP:

Therefore, brethren, since we have full freedom and confidence to enter into the [Holy of] Holies [by the power and virtue] in the blood of Jesus.

By this fresh (new) and living way which He initiated and dedicated and opened for us

through the separating curtain (veil of the Holy of Holies), that is, through His flesh.

Jesus entered the place where no sin could go. He had already carried all our sin to the Cross and to Hell, paying the price with His own blood. But then He arose and ascended to the heavenly Holy of Holies, where He sprinkled His own blood on the mercy seat of God once and for all for us.

If most people were God, I believe they would have stopped right there. They would have let Jesus be the only One Who could enter the Holy of Holies. But God never stops halfway. In verses 21-22 AMP, He invites us to enter the Holy of Holies for ourselves:

And since we have [such] a great and wonderful and noble Priest [Who rules] over the house of God, let us all come forward and draw near with true (honest and sincere) hearts in unqualified assurance and absolute conviction engendered by faith (by that leaning of the entire human personality on God in absolute trust and confidence in His power, wisdom, and goodness), having our hearts sprinkled and purified from a guilty (evil) conscience and our bodies cleansed with pure water.

God invites you to come into His throne room where no sin can come. How are you going to do that if you're not perfect? Only by the blood of Jesus. By pleading the blood of Jesus you may confidently approach the throne of God with clean hands and a pure heart. This has a greater meaning to us than we have realized.

The Devil Can't Cross the Blood Line

When I first began to gain an understanding about the blood of Jesus, I would hear Billye Brim say, "When you plead the blood of Jesus, you draw a circle around your home and your family, and the devil can't cross that blood line."

Well, that made sense to me, and I knew it was true. But I wanted to know *why*. Why is it that when you plead the blood the devil can't cross that line? I believed it was true but I still wanted to understand why.

So I began searching the Word, and the Lord gave me some answers to my questions—answers that all centered around pleading the blood of Jesus.

When you plead the blood of Jesus, you enter the Holy of Holies by the power and the virtue in that blood; sin and death can't go there because they can't exist in the presence of God. You live in Jesus' righteousness. The knowledge of that truth begins to build up on the inside of you as you speak forth words of faith: "I'm living in the righteousness of God today. I'm walking in His footsteps today. The enemy cannot bring tragedy to my family. He cannot bring sickness or death to my home. God judges me the way He would judge Jesus. I'm pure and clean because of the blood of Jesus!"

And it doesn't stop there. God hasn't just provided the way for you to *enter* the Holy of Holies; He wants you to live your life there!

That is the key. After all, the presence of God resides on the inside of you. You don't have to live your life outside the Holy of Holies just because it's time to go to the grocery store. You and your children can live every aspect of your lives in God's presence. You never have to leave His presence—but it's only because of the blood of Jesus.

So what are you doing when you plead the blood of Jesus over yourself, your spouse and your children each morning? *You are placing yourselves in the Holy of Holies, where the devil cannot come.* He cannot cross that line, because on the other side of that line is the presence of God, and the devil, his plans and his devices are instantly destroyed!

That excites me so much, because in this day and age we're living in, no physical location is a sanctuary. Schools are no longer sanctuaries. Even a church is not a sanctuary—unless its people understand how to build a hedge around it by pleading the blood of Jesus.

There is only one true sanctuary, and that is before the throne of God. And it is God Himself who issues us an invitation to draw near:

> **Let us then fearlessly and confidently and boldly draw near to the throne of grace (the throne of God's unmerited favor to us sinners), that we may receive grace to help in good times for every need [appropriate help and well-timed help, coming just when we need it].**
>
> **Hebrews 4:16 AMP**

First of all, understand this: This Scripture is *not* talking about approaching the throne of grace once we get to heaven. We aren't going to need mercy for our failures after we go home to be with the Lord. All our needs and desires will already be met. No, this Scripture is our promise for life on this earth.

So where is the help we need? Only in the Holy of Holies, the throne of grace. By the blood of Jesus, we can approach God's throne with fearless confidence. That kind of bold confidence is what many of us have been missing—even those of us who know how to plead the blood. But it is a necessary ingredient for living our entire lives in God's sanctuary by faith.

Hearing Wisdom in the Holy of Holies

Living our lives in God's presence provides us with such a wonderful sense of security. That is where our answers are. That is where wisdom is.

Every morning when I pray with my children we plead the blood of Jesus over our lives. We charge our angels to go before us to protect us in all our ways. And lately we've been adding something else to our prayers. Now we also pray for wisdom.

The Bible says that wisdom *cries out.* (Proverbs 1:20.) Well, I want my family to be in a position to hear God's wisdom when He speaks it to us. So I say every morning, "Wisdom cries out to us, and we listen and obey."

I find myself hearing the voice of God better when I live in the Holy of Holies every day by the blood of Jesus. I make better decisions, and so do my children.

For instance, one day my son Max came in and said about a certain brand of toys, "Mommy, I'm going to have to throw them all away. They don't honor God, and they don't further my ministry."

Now, I had been about to take those toys away from Max because I had been sensing in my spirit that they weren't good. But I didn't have to do that because my eight-year-old son heard wisdom from God—exactly what we had been praying for!

Max dwells in the Holy of Holies, even though he doesn't fully comprehend that. But while he was living in God's presence, he heard the Lord say to him, "That doesn't honor Me."

My husband, Win, and I have trained our children to obey. So when Max heard that, he threw those toys away. He didn't think about how much they had cost him. He just threw it in the trash and left it there, and he hasn't regretted it a moment since.

As some of my children became teenagers, my desire to protect them and to know that they are able to hear wisdom grew in me. I'm constantly talking to the Lord about my teenagers. I'm so glad they can live with Jesus in His home, the throne room of God. That's where they will find wisdom. That's where the devil cannot go to attack them.

When your children are in the presence of God, they are keeping company with the Wisdom of the ages. God will give them the wisdom to make right decisions, whether it is about peer pressure, pornography, cigarettes, alcohol or premarital sex. Whatever the issue, God has wisdom for your children to protect them from the temptations of this world and the devil's evil strategies.

But that divine wisdom resides in the Holy of Holies, and the only way your children can live there is by the blood of Jesus. When you and your children plead His blood, you enter the Holy of Holies, where God is ready to impart as much protection, favor and grace to you as He would to Jesus Himself.

As a parent, you must also hear wisdom in the Holy of Holies if you want your children fully protected. There will be many times you will have to make a decision concerning your children and you won't know for sure what to do. Thank God, you have His promise that He will give you wisdom liberally when you ask Him for it!

> **If any of you is deficient in wisdom, let him ask of the giving God [Who gives] to everyone liberally and ungrudgingly, without reproaching or faultfinding, and it will be given him.**
>
> **James 1:5 AMP**

All you have to do is pray, "Lord, You said You would give me wisdom liberally and that I was to let Your peace rule and reign in my heart (Colossians 3:15 AMP). So I ask for wisdom and peace from You regarding the right way to go in this matter."

I can't remember a time when I prayed like that and didn't get an almost immediate answer from the Lord. For instance, one time some people wanted my daughter to go somewhere with them, but I didn't have a peace about it in my heart. I struggled with what to do because I didn't want to offend these people.

I have found that we usually say we don't know what to do when we really do; we just don't want to do it. But we need to lay aside all the circumstances and the pressures that surround us and listen for God's wisdom to show us the way to go.

If you are listening to wisdom, none of those things matter. Your objective is to hear what God is trying to say to you so your children can stay protected and blessed. If you let the pressure of natural circumstances get to you, you may miss the voice of God.

Anyway, I talked to a friend about this situation with my daughter. I told her, "I just don't know what to do."

"I bet you do know," she said.

"No, I don't," I protested.

"All right, then, ask God for wisdom," she replied.

So right there, I prayed, asking God for wisdom according to His promise in James 1:5. Then my friend said, "Now, all circumstances aside, do you have peace about letting her go?"

"No, I don't," I answered.

There was the wisdom I needed! It was the answer the Holy Spirit had been trying to get across to me all along. But why was I able to hear wisdom when it was crying out to me? Because I placed myself in a position to hear.

Wash Your Hands in Innocence

This helps us understand why the devil has been able to gain so much access to Christians in his strategies to kill, steal and destroy. Many believers haven't been living where they're supposed to be living!

You should make it your goal to abide in God's presence continually. His throne room should be your home.

In Psalm 26:6 AMP, the psalmist David gives us a better understanding of what is required to make the altar of God, the Holy of Holies, our home: **I will wash my hands in innocence, and go about Your altar, O Lord.**

We saw earlier in Psalm 24:4 that we can only draw near to God with clean hands and a sincere, pure heart. We can't just act any way we want to and then expect to get away with it by pleading the blood. We have to live right and do the right things.

In Psalm 26:6 AMP, David makes this same point when he says, **I will wash my hands in innocence.** But how do we go about washing our hands in innocence? *By appropriating the blood of Jesus to our lives.*

We are citizens of heaven, not of this earth. But it is only by washing ourselves with the blood of Jesus that we can plead innocent to the accusations of the enemy. God has given us the ability to "go about His altar," living continually in His presence. However, we must get there by washing our hands in innocence through the cleansing blood of the Lamb.

In John 6:53-56, Jesus talked about something else we must do in order to live our lives in the Holy of Holies. Not only are we to wash ourselves in the blood of Jesus, but in this passage of Scripture, Jesus says we are to *drink* His blood.

That must have been a real shock to the disciples when Jesus told them that! Think about it. They had been taught all their lives that they were never to partake of blood. That was forbidden under Levitical law. But Jesus said, **For my flesh is meat indeed, and my blood is drink indeed. He that eateth my flesh, and drinketh my blood, dwelleth in me, and I in him** (John 6:55,56).

So how do we go about obeying this unusual command from the Master? Well, consider the difference between drinking and bathing in water. When we bathe in water, we use it to cleanse us. But when we drink water, we take it in, appropriating its refreshing properties to revive and bring new life to our physical bodies.

In the same way, we have been cleansed by the blood of Jesus, but we shouldn't stop there. We must *drink* it—appropriating its life-giving, protecting power to every aspect of our lives. And just as we have to partake of water every day in order to survive physically, we must do the same with the blood of Jesus to protect our children and ourselves.

Standing in the Protection
of God's 'Even Place'

Let's go back to Psalm 26 for a moment. In verse 12 AMP, David describes what life is like as he "goes about" the altar of God: **My foot stands on an even place; in the congregations will I bless the Lord.**

What a promise God has given you in this verse! Your family can go through life standing on an even place. That's talking about the habitation of God's house—a secure sanctuary with no unexpected bumps to make you stumble and fall. That place is the Holy of Holies. Nowhere can you find a place more "even" or secure than that!

Now, you may miss it and go over a bump of your own making. But even then, the Lord will see to it that you and your family are protected as you apply the blood of Jesus to your lives.

God knows who you are. He knows what you're up against. And He knows that you are changing, day by day, into the image of His Son. So He has made a way through the blood of Jesus for you to win as thoroughly as you would if you were already perfect! Your family can win 100 percent as you are faithful to keep them standing on that even place through the power of the blood of Jesus.

David had no higher priority than to dwell in that even place all the days of his life. In Psalm 27:4 AMP, he said this:

One thing have I asked of the Lord, that will I seek, inquire for, and [insistently] require: that I may dwell in the house of the Lord [in His presence] all the days of my life, to behold and gaze upon the beauty [the sweet attractiveness and the delightful loveliness] of the Lord and to meditate, consider, and inquire in His temple.

David had to go to a physical temple in order to dwell in God's presence. But when Jesus died on the cross, the veil separating the Holy of Holies in the temple was ripped open, and the Holy Spirit came out to dwell within God's people.

Now we are the temple of the living God. (2 Corinthians 6:16.) Now we can enjoy the sweetness and the protection of His presence as we dwell in that even place by the blood of Jesus:

The secret [of the sweet, satisfying companionship] of the Lord have they who fear (revere and worship) Him, and He will show them His covenant and reveal to them its [deep, inner] meaning. My eyes are ever toward the Lord, for He will pluck my feet out of the net.

Psalm 25:14,15 AMP

God will pluck your family's feet out of the net that the enemy has laid for them. Why? Because your eyes are ever toward the Lord. You are trusting Him for deliverance from the "day of trouble" spoken of in Psalm 27:5 AMP:

For in the day of trouble He will hide me in His shelter; in the secret place of His tent will He hide me; He will set me high upon a rock.

When you plead the blood of Jesus, you are laying down your pride and your own ability to protect yourself, your spouse and your children. Instead, you are picking up the ability of God, putting yourself in a position where God can move on your behalf to hide you and your family from trouble.

Notice that all these verses in the book of Psalms talk about being protected as you stand continually in the presence of God. I'm telling you, my friend, *that is the key.*

But you and your children don't just live in God's presence automatically. You live there by daily pleading the blood of Jesus over your lives in faith. As you do, you put your family in a position to live each day in the sanctuary the devil can't touch—the heavenly Holy of Holies!

We Have Our Part to Play

Now look at Hebrews 10:23 AMP:

> **So let us seize and hold fast and retain without wavering the hope we cherish and confess and our acknowledgement of it, for He Who promised is reliable (sure) and faithful to His word.**

Notice again that even though we have full freedom to enter the Holy of Holies, it isn't automatic. We have to *seize, obtain, draw near, lay hold, enter in and hold fast to the hope we cherish.* We have to *confess* and *acknowledge* with the words of our mouth that eternal hope. We do that by pleading the blood of Jesus. That is our confession and acknowledgment of what He has done for us.

Verse 23 AMP also says that **He Who promised is reliable (sure) and faithful to His word.** People always say, "God is so faithful to His people." But this verse says God is faithful to His *Word.* He has, in a sense, limited Himself to helping us to the extent that we comply with His Word.

God is as faithful as He can be to us. He is as faithful as we *let* Him be. He is always doing 100 percent of what He can do for us. Thankfully, He endeavors to teach us when we mess up. And He is certainly the God of a second chance (and third and fourth, etc.!). Even so, if we want to live a victorious life we have to speak the Word, receive the Word and appropriate the Word on a daily basis. If we will be faithful to God's Word, He can be fully faithful to us. But if we're constantly speaking death, He can't be faithful to that. For instance, if we're speaking lack, there is very little life God can bring to our finances. Understand, it works the same way with protection and safety.

On the other hand, as we speak what God's Word says over the situations we face in life, He can fix things fast! He *can* and He *will* because He *wants* to!

It is actually good news to know that God has tied Himself to His Word. That means all you have to do is say what He says, and the outcome is assured. God will be faithful to perform what He has promised in your life. He will meet your needs. He will protect your children. He is going to do what He has said He would do.

God will never go back on His sovereign decision to give you a choice. You have to decide whether or not you will do your part to receive His promise of protection. But God will also never go back on that promise when you plead the blood of Jesus and stand in His righteousness.

If you fulfill the requirements for divine protection, you never need to worry that God might not fulfill His promise to protect you and your family. He is faithful to His Word. And to the extent that you are faithful to God's Word, you can have all that His Word says you can have.

CHAPTER 5

The Absolute Certainty
of Divine Protection

Here is an absolute guarantee: *There is no more certain place to be than in the presence of God. And when I say certain, I mean safe, secure and assured.* You can count on it. Even if the Lord prompts you to go minister to someone in a hospital filled with deadly, contagious diseases, you can go with confidence and peace. Why? Because you know you are walking in God's presence, and in that divine presence is certain, supernatural protection.

Whenever the Lord says with great certainty in His Word that you can possess something, it should be very difficult for the devil to take that promise away from you. On the other hand, it may be harder for you to be confident if you are praying for something that isn't specifically promised in the Word. In that case, you need a strong inner knowing from the Holy Spirit that the petition you have asked for is yours to claim.

You are a covenant person. Therefore, you should be confident that God will perform His promise of protection for you as you stand in His presence by faith.

Hebrews 6:19 AMP talks about a hope that helps us enter the absolute certainty and security of God's presence:

> **[Now] we have this [hope] as a sure and stead-fast anchor of the soul [it cannot slip and it cannot break down under whoever steps out upon it—a hope] that reaches farther and enters into [the very certainty of the Presence] within the veil.**

Let's read the two previous verses to find out what that hope is:

> **Accordingly God also, in His desire to show more convincingly and beyond doubt to those who were to inherit the promise the unchangeableness of His purpose and plan, intervened (mediated) with an oath.**

> **This was so that, by two unchangeable things (His promise and His oath) in which it is impossible for God ever to prove false or deceive us, we who have fled [to Him] for refuge might have mighty indwelling**

**strength and strong encouragement to grasp
and hold fast the hope appointed for us and
set before [us].**

Hebrews 6:17,18 AMP

Verse 17 is talking about the oath God made to Abraham, the father of our faith. To show Abraham "convincingly and beyond doubt" that what He had promised to him was absolutely certain, God intervened with an oath made by blood. Thus, by those two unchangeable things—God's promise and His oath made by blood—we, too, can grasp and hold fast to the hope set before us.

God wants you to grasp the hope He has given you through His promise of protection. The blood of Jesus can work in your life so much more powerfully when you are fully persuaded.

You don't get very far when you are wavering in your faith, always wondering, *Is pleading the blood of Jesus going to accomplish anything? Are my children really going to be delivered in the midst of danger just because I do this every day?* That's why God wants you to be convinced beyond a shadow of a doubt that He will faithfully keep you and your children safe from all harm.

God has laid out in His Word all the provisions of His covenant with us, including supernatural deliverance and protection. Then He made an oath by the blood of Jesus, giving us the mighty indwelling strength and strong encouragement to firmly grasp hold of this hope that has been set before us.

Verse 19 AMP says that this hope is **a sure and steadfast anchor of the soul.** Your soul—which is made up of your mind, your will and your emotions—is the part of you that needs anchoring because it is the arena where the devil most often attacks. If it weren't for the battle that goes on with your thought life and your roller-coaster emotions, it would be much easier for you to make your flesh fall in line with your spirit man. Therefore, the soul is the part of you that must be consciously and continually renewed and submitted to God and His Word.

For instance, as you live your daily life, sometimes fear or worry can attack your mind and cause you to waver from the Word. That's when you have to anchor your tumultuous emotions by telling your soul, "Be quiet! I'm acting according to what the Word of God says, not according to circumstances."

Your hope lies in the oath God made by the blood of His Son to perform every promise in His Word. You have that hope as a steadfast anchor for your soul. That hope cannot slip or break, no matter who tries to step on it. It's a hope that reaches far into your heart, into the very certainty of the presence of God within the veil. It is something you can literally lay your hands on and put into force, knowing with absolute certainty that God will do exactly what He said He would do for you through the power in the blood of Jesus.

Nothing Missing, Nothing Broken

I want to go further in the Word to "prove my case" that God's promise to protect us from every calamity is certain and sure. Let's start by looking at Romans 5:1 AMP:

> **Therefore, since we are justified (acquitted, declared righteous, and given a right standing with God) through faith, let us [grasp the fact that we] have [the peace of reconciliation to hold and to enjoy] peace with God through our Lord Jesus Christ (the Messiah, the Anointed One).**

Paul uses a lot of legal words in this chapter. For instance, in this verse he says that we have been *justified* or *acquitted* before the Judge of all.

I want to say something about this concept of justification. One of the biggest robbers of the Church today is the making of excuses. When you make an excuse for the shape your life is in, you are trying to justify yourself. In doing so, you take your justification out of the hands of the only One Who can actually make you righteous and blameless. You'll be excused all right—excused from protection and blessings!

When people go through a tragedy and say, "It must have been God's will," I believe that qualifies as an excuse. In saying the tragedy was God's will, they excuse themselves from taking any responsibility and deny the possibility that they may have failed to fulfill a divine requirement. Instead, they put all the responsibility on God.

People who live like that forfeit so much of God's power operating in their lives because they won't allow Him to justify them. Don't make that same mistake! Do whatever you have to in order to *grasp* the fact that you have peace with God to hold and enjoy.

(By the way, have you noticed that God often uses words like "grasp" and "hold" in this type of context? These truths are really something He wants us to get ahold of!)

In revealing to us the root meaning of the Hebrew word *Shalom*, Billye Brim has forever changed the way I read God's Word! Shalom means nothing missing, nothing broken. Those few words speak volumes. Peace is literally living with *nothing missing and nothing broken* in your life. That's God's way. He has given you and your family everything you could ever need or require to be completely whole and successful in life.

Every need you might have to accomplish every single thing God has ever asked you to do has been set aside in abundance for your peace and your wholeness. There should never be a time when you or your family members are not whole. But how do you reach that place of peace and wholeness? Only by the blood of Jesus.

If you look throughout God's Word, you will see that wherever things were missing, God replaced them with better things. Wherever things were broken, He fixed them or gave something brand new.

That's what God wants to do for you as well. By the blood of Jesus, you have peace and total reconciliation with Him. He will guard and guide you and your family in every area of life so that nothing is ever left missing or broken. Regardless of the calamities that may befall the earth—the shootings, bombings, airplane wrecks, earthquakes and tornadoes—God says, "Grasp firmly the peace you have with Me through the blood of My Son. Nothing need ever be broken or missing in the lives of you or your family."

Divine Protection:
More Certain Than Being Born Again?

It's easy to say, "Oh, I do believe that God will protect my family from all harm." But you need be so sure of that fact that you immediately respond in faith when your family is attacked by the enemy.

How can you be that certain of God's protection? Let's read on in Romans 5:2 AMP:

Through Him also we have [our] access (entrance, introduction) by faith into this grace (state of God's favor) in which we [firmly and safely] stand. And let us rejoice and exult in our hope of experiencing and enjoying the glory of God.

Through Jesus we have access into the Holy of Holies. We stand firmly and safely in this state of God's favor and grace. It is a place where no matter what the devil tries to do, God looks at us and says, "I judge you the way I would judge Jesus. I see you as possessing all the good qualities Jesus possesses. I am just as ready to move on your behalf as I am ready to move on the behalf of My Son."

That's what happens when you stand in God's grace and favor. As Isaiah 54:17 says, no weapon formed against you will prosper in that place because you, by virtue of His righteousness, stand firmly and safely in the sanctuary of His presence.

But your access into God's presence is by faith. That means you have to exercise your faith. You have to aggressively lay hold of your right to enjoy continual access to God's throne just because the Word says it is true.

Now let's look at what verse 9 AMP says:

Therefore, since we are now justified (acquitted, made righteous, and brought into right

relationship with God) by Christ's blood, how much more [certain is it that] we shall be saved by Him from the indignation and wrath of God.

First of all, let's see what Paul is referring to in this verse when he says, "the indignation and wrath of God."

Paul is talking about the judgments that come as a result of sin on this earth. God is 100 percent against sin. He is as far from sin as He can get. But although His wrath against sin will one day be poured out, that isn't happening now. When it does, people will definitely know it. However, we as believers won't be here to see it.

So what is Paul talking about when he says we will be saved from the indignation and the wrath of God? He is saying that God will deliver us from paying the price for sin—death. That would include all that the devil could bring against you.

Now let's look at the profound statement this verse makes about how certain of God's covenant promise of protection is for you and your family. Paul says here you should be more certain that God would deliver you from a dangerous situation, from tragedy and loss, from sickness and disease or from anything else the enemy might throw at you than you were certain He would save you from sin in the first place!

Let's see what else the Word says about this.

For if while we were enemies we were reconciled to God through the death of His Son, it is much more [certain], now that we are reconciled, that we shall be saved (daily delivered from sin's dominion) through His [resurrection] life.

Romans 5:10 AMP

He said it! If God would deliver you while you were still His enemy, wouldn't He do even more for you now that you're His child?

Suppose I asked you, "Are you certain you're saved?"

You would probably say, "Well, of course, I'm saved!"

"Well, I don't know. I don't really think you're saved."

"Yes, I am!" you'd say indignantly. "I'm going to heaven. Jesus is my Lord."

More than likely, you are this certain that you are a child of God. But according this Scripture, you should be even more certain that God will *daily* deliver you and your children from sin's dominion than you are that you are saved.

But what *is* "sin's dominion"? It is the judgment or the price that is attached to sin. That includes all the tragedies, killings and natural disasters that take place on this earth. It includes poverty, train wrecks, car accidents, and every sickness and disease.

All these things fall under the category of sin's dominion because the wages of sin is death. And God says that He will daily deliver you and your children from them all. Because of the blood of Jesus and His righteousness, you don't *deserve* the dominion or the recompense of sin.

God has provided a way to deliver you from judgment through the blood and the resurrection life of His Son. That should be an absolute certainty in your heart. There should be no question about it. The devil should never be able to come in and convince you that God is not going to protect your family. You have God's Word on it, and it is impossible for Him to lie.

A Way of Escape

We have established as an absolute certainty that God will protect and deliver us from sin's dominion. It just thrills me every time I think about that. So many of us have thought we were still subject to unexpected tragedies and calamities. We hoped God would protect us, but it wasn't all that certain to us.

But now we're beginning to see how the grace of God works to bring us divine protection. Grace is able to work for us because we're in the footsteps of Jesus. We stand in His righteousness. It has nothing to do with our own goodness or righteousness. (If you didn't lead a very righteous life in the past, that is probably very good news to you!)

Verse 12 AMP goes on to describe where we all were before God made a way of escape for us through Jesus:

> **Therefore, as sin came into the world through one man, and death as the result of sin, so death spread to all men, [no one being able to stop it or to escape its power] because all men sinned.**

Before Jesus, sinful people didn't have a way to escape the power of death except for the temporary fix God put into place through animal sacrifice. But now there *is* a way of escape. We can escape every form of sin and death at work in the earth today through the blood of Jesus.

Death Will No Longer 'Hold Sway'

One day I was studying the Word on the blood of Jesus, and the Lord caught me on the first part of Romans 5:14 AMP. It says, **Yet *death held sway* from Adam to Moses....**

Death held sway from Adam to Moses. That phrase caught my attention. I didn't know what it meant, so I thought, *I know! I'll call my dad.*

My dad, Kenneth Copeland, is my ever-ready "Bible encyclopedia." But when I called him, I found out he had gone fishing!

Since I couldn't ask Dad, I thought, *I guess I'll just have to ask the Lord.* (The Lord is the One I should have asked in the first place!)

I said, "All right, Lord, what does this mean? You obviously want to tell me something."

To my surprise, the Holy Spirit answered me immediately with one simple word: *"Passover."*

Death held sway from Adam to Moses. But on the night of that first Passover, death lost its control.

Before the first Passover, death held the cards, so to speak. No one could escape its power. Everything on this earth was going death's way. Death *held sway* until that night when God's people applied the blood of the Passover lamb to their doorposts. Death could no longer push its way in where it didn't belong; it had to pass over the Israelites' homes that were protected by the blood.

The same thing is true today. In the lives of people who don't know the Lord, death still holds sway. That is the way the wind of judgment is blowing.

But the Lamb of God shed His blood for you and your family. And if you will just apply it to the doorposts of your life, death has to pass over.

On the other hand, if you don't take part in that Passover spiritually by receiving the protection that Jesus' blood bought for us, death will still hold sway in your life. Death is still the direction your natural life is headed toward unless you get off that path by the delivering power of the blood.

Imagine What It Was Like

Now I want you to take a moment to imagine yourself back in the days when the children of Israel were in slavery. I want you to see yourself and your family there on the night Moses said the Lord would lead His people out of bondage.

You pick up the hyssop branch and apply the blood of the Passover lamb to your door and side posts, just as God commanded Moses. The blood is on your doorposts, and you, your spouse and your children are gathered together behind that door. You hold your youngest child in your arms.

You know that your sister is in her home down the street. Her family has also applied the blood of their Passover lamb to their door.

You and your family are sitting together at the table, recounting what God has done for your people in the past, enjoying your time together behind the door of your home. All of a sudden, you begin to hear weeping and crying. Children are dying in their mothers' arms. The mothers wail,

"Oh, my baby, my baby!" but there is nothing they can do except cry in agony.

The screams are horrendous. All that horror and grief is right on the other side of that door. Every member of your family can hear the effects of death outside.

Then you look around the room at your own family, and you know with unshakable certainty that they will come through this night unscathed, unharmed and secure. There is no question or doubt in your mind about it. You don't have one moment of fear or anxiety, wondering what might happen to your children.

You realize that because of the promise God gave you—because you obeyed His instructions to put that blood on your doorposts—death is not coming into your home. It is going to pass by because it *can't* come in.

You look at your little baby snuggled contentedly in your arms, and you know this little one is protected. You look at your children and your spouse sitting around the table, and you know they're safe from all harm. Death may surround you, but it can't touch you or your family because of the blood of the Passover lamb.

What security, what peace—that is real "blessed assurance." But think about it—that is just a *fraction* of what we have in Jesus today. The children of Israel were delivered from death by the blood of an animal. But as the Word says, *how much more* does the blood of Jesus deliver us from every form of sin's dominion?

We see mothers crying on television newscasts because their children have died. We see people wailing in grief over the loss of their loved ones during an earthquake or a hurricane. None of these tragedies make any sense. To the world, they seem inescapable.

But thank God, we don't live in "the land of Egypt"! There is "light in the land of Goshen." We live behind the blood of Jesus in the Holy of Holies! That precious blood protects us and delivers us from all evil. All we have to do is apply the blood of Jesus to the doorposts of our lives on a daily basis.

As we learn to appropriate and honor the blood of Jesus, we and our families will be able to walk through life just as certain of our protection as the Israelites were when they sat behind their blood-stained doors and death passed them by.

The Blood of Jesus Seals Us in God's Grace

The Israelites could have chosen to open their doors and go outside on that Passover night. If they had, they would have still been God's people. But remember, the blood of the Passover lamb represented the propitiation, or the atonement, for their sin. If they had left their homes, they would have put themselves outside the protection of that blood where death could go after them.

The Hebrew word meaning propitiation or atonement doesn't just mean to *cover* sin. The root word actually refers to *bitumen* or *pitch,* a substance akin to tar that Noah used to seal and waterproof the ark.[2]

The pitch covering Noah's ark sealed *out* the rain and sealed the occupants of the ark *inside* God's protection. In the same way, the blood of Jesus doesn't just cover sin; it actually acts as a seal between us and sin. It seals sin *out* and seals us *in* the grace of God.

The blood of Jesus seals you and your family in the Holy of Holies with all the good things of God. At the same time, it seals out all the bad things the devil wants to throw at you.

I want to take you back to an earlier passage in Romans for a moment. I want to show you a picture of the world as we know it today. It is a very fitting description of that which the blood of Jesus has sealed us from.

It is so funny to me when people talk about the Bible being irrelevant. They must not know what it says. The truth is, the Word continually updates itself and is always current. Just look at what Romans 3:10-18 AMP says:

---

[2] James Strong, "Hebrew Dictionary of the Old Testament," The New Strong's Exhaustive Concordance of the Bible (Nashville: Thomas Nelson Publishers, 1985), #3722

As it is written, None is righteous, just and truthful and conscientious, no, not one. No one understands [no one intelligently discerns or comprehends]; no one seeks out God. All have turned aside; together they have gone wrong and have become unprofitable and worthless; no one does right, not even one!

Their throat is a yawning grave; they use their tongues to deceive (to mislead and to deal treacherously). The venom of asps is beneath their lips. Their mouth is full of cursing and bitterness. Their feet are swift to shed blood.

Destruction [as it dashes them to pieces] and misery mark their ways. And they have no experience of the way of peace [they know nothing about peace, for a peaceful way they do not even recognize]. There is no [reverential] fear of God before their eyes.

That is such a good description of the world today! People in the world think they have the answers and that Christians are foolish. But the truth is, the worldly people are the ones who are foolish—so foolish, in fact, that they don't even recognize the truth when they see it!

This passage describes the perilous road to judgment. But, praise God, we can get off that road! We don't have to be there when judgment is taking place. And if we are in a place where it is happening, we don't have to be part of it. We are not citizens of the world as this passage describes. We are citizens of heaven, sealed in the grace of God through the blood of Jesus!

Now let's read verses 21-26 in the *King James Version:*

> **But now the righteousness of God** [or the ability to stand in God's presence in the Holy of Holies] **without the law is manifested, being witnessed by the law and the prophets; Even the righteousness of God which is by faith of Jesus Christ unto all and upon all them that believe: for there is no difference:**
>
> **For all have sinned, and come short of the glory of God; Being justified freely by his grace through the redemption that is in Christ Jesus: Whom God hath set forth to be a propitiation** [a cover or a seal] *through faith in his blood,* **to declare his righteousness for the remission of sins that are past, through the forbearance of God; To declare, I say, at this time his righteousness: that he might be just, and the justifier of him which believeth in Jesus.**

If you want Jesus to be your Justifier, you must declare with the words of your mouth that He is your Justifier by virtue of His blood. Then He will be your Justifier. He will be the One Who declares you are innocent by His blood.

The righteousness of God is what the blood of Jesus paid for. Therefore, your justification—the right to live in the Holy of Holies, safe from the effects of judgment on this earth—is accomplished only through faith in His blood.

Stay in Your Sanctuary

We have a sanctuary that is far more powerful than the blood of the Passover lamb that was put on the Israelites' doors. We have a sure and certain sanctuary in the powerful blood of Jesus.

Doesn't it just thrill you to know that in this age of uncertainty? I mean, you may be sure of what *you're* going to do each day, but who knows what the person driving in the car next to you or the person walking into the post office behind you is going to do?

Praise the Lord, it doesn't matter what anyone else does—you can live in your sanctuary. No matter what kind of situation you find yourself in, just stay in that sanctuary. Wherever your children go, keep them safe within that sanctuary. Teach them to stay in the Holy of Holies. God will even help them pick their friends. He will see to it that they are protected and where they need to be.

Come boldly before God's throne by virtue of the blood. Walk in the footsteps of Jesus into the Holy of Holies, and ask for righteous judgment. No matter what is going on all around you, fix your heart on the certainty of God's protection as you plead the blood of Jesus over your family every day. Chaos and judgment may swirl just outside your door, but you and your children will stay safe in your sanctuary, protected by the blood of the Lamb!

Keep Your Heart Fixed

Psalm 112:7-8 AMP describes someone whose heart is fixed on God and His Word, a person who is absolutely certain of his protection within the sanctuary of God:

> **He shall not be afraid of evil tidings; his heart is firmly fixed, trusting (leaning on and being confident) in the Lord. His heart is established and steady, he will not be afraid while he waits to see his desire established upon his adversaries.**

This really describes my family during those times the enemy has tried to come against us. We truly are not afraid of evil tidings.

I don't say that in a prideful way at all; it's just the truth. For instance, my daughter Jenny was in a car accident when she was 18 months old. Paramedics said she was unresponsive at the scene and they didn't expect her to make it. But the Lord supernaturally delivered Jenny. In just a few days, she was out of the hospital!

How did that happen? While we were in the hospital with Jenny, we kept our hearts fixed on God's covenant promises and the power of the blood. Rather than yielding to fear, we waited to see our desire established on our enemy, the devil. We knew what the outcome would be, but it was the blood covenant we had with God that made us secure.

The blood of Jesus was shed for your salvation and deliverance from sin's dominion. It is your faith in the Word of God and the blood of Jesus that makes you unafraid when challenges arise. You can do anything God asks you to do. You can go anywhere God asks you to go—as long as you are certain of your covenant with Him.

Since Jenny's accident, my family has learned so much more about applying the blood of Jesus to our lives. Today we are *far* ahead of where we were spiritually when that happened.

However, too many Christians are *not* covenant-minded; instead, they react in fear to any type of evil tidings. When bad things happen, they become fearful that something similar will happen to them.

For instance, when a shooting occurred at a Fort Worth church, it scared a lot of Christians. They started asking, "If I

can't send my kids to church and know that they are protected, where can I send them?"

The truth is, you can't send your children anywhere and
know for certain that they are protected unless you walk by
faith in your covenant and in the blood of Jesus. On the
other hand, if you live this way—if you become covenant-
minded and learn to stay in your sanctuary by the blood of
Jesus—your heart will become fixed. You will know beyond
a shadow of a doubt that God's promise of protection is not
a vague hope, but an established fact.

In contrast, Psalm 112:10 AMP describes the way a person
who doesn't know the Lord responds to adversity:

> **The wicked men will see it and be grieved and
> angered, he will gnash his teeth and disappear
> [in despair]; the desire of the wicked shall
> perish and come to nothing.**

Have you ever seen unsaved people deal with a difficult
situation the way this verse describes? I have. For instance, I
have watched the different reactions of unsaved parents
whose children were ill with a terminal disease. Some of
them were very angry; some of them were upset; and some of
them just sat in despair with no clue about what to do. They
just waited for the doctor to tell them what was going to
happen to their child.

Lacking a Savior, these parents had no recourse but to accept whatever the enemy would throw at them. Put this Scripture together with Proverbs 12:13 which says that the wicked is snared by the transgression of his lips. He has an evil heart of unbelief. When something tragic occurs, what can he do? He will see it (the evil tidings) and be grieved and mad, but his desire for deliverance will come to nothing. He is without hope and without God in the world as in Ephesians 2:12.

On the other hand, the desire of the covenant man is to see his adversary, the devil, defeated. The covenant man just waits expecting to see his desired outcome. He knows it is coming; he is confident that he stands in a place of favor and grace before the throne of God. His heart is fixed.

Does that describe you? If you can't answer with a confident *yes,* it's time to work on becoming a covenant-minded believer! Fix your heart on the Word and on the power in the blood of Jesus until all doubts in your mind are erased forever. No matter what is going on around you, keep your family in the sanctuary of God's presence by pleading the blood of Jesus every day.

Remember, there is no more certain place to be than in the presence of God—secure in your covenant with Him.

Chapter 6

It's Your Choice!

∽o∾

Now that you know about the certainty of God's promise of protection, you can probably understand better what I'm about to tell you: *It's entirely your choice whether or not your family is protected.*

The world may tell you otherwise. Even certain religious people will tell you it is *God's* choice and not yours whether or not your family is protected from harm. But that just isn't what the Word says. You have a big part to play in ensuring that you and your children dwell safely in God's sanctuary.

Do Martyrs Have a Choice?

As I have gone from place to place teaching on this subject of protecting your family by the blood of Jesus, one question people have asked me is this: "If those who were martyred through the years couldn't choose to be protected from physical harm and death, why can we choose?"

I thought that was a good question, so I began praying about it. "What about that, Lord?" I asked. "Why can we choose to be protected, yet the martyrs couldn't choose the same thing?"

The Lord led me to Hebrews 11 for my answer. Now, I had read this chapter many, many times before. I knew it was the "hall of faith," the chapter where God talks about the faith exploits of the mighty men and women of the Bible. But this time I saw something I had never seen before. Let me show you what I mean.

> **And what shall I more say? for the time would fail me to tell of Gedeon, and of Barak, and of Samson, and of Jephthae; of David also, and Samuel, and of the prophets: Who through faith subdued kingdoms, wrought righteousness, obtained promises, stopped the mouths of lions.**
>
> **Quenched the violence of fire, escaped the edge of the sword, out of weakness were made strong, waxed valiant in fight, turned to flight the armies of the aliens.**
>
> **Hebrews 11:32,33**

This sounds kind of familiar, doesn't it? It sounds like some of the violence going on in the world today! Back then, people faced swords and wild lions. Today, people face other dangers.

If the writer of Hebrews lived in these modern days, he might write, "They quenched the violence of gunfire and escaped the threat of bombings and terrorists." These are the types of modern perils we want our children to be delivered from. We want to know that they're continually protected from calamity and evil, no matter what may be happening around them.

Then verse 35 talks about those who were martyrs: **Women received their dead raised to life again: and others were tortured,** *not accepting deliverance;* **that they might obtain a better resurrection.** Notice that it says these people were tortured because they *didn't accept* deliverance.

In other words, if martyrdom is what a believer wants, he can have that. The Bible says that martyrs will have a better resurrection. But there is a lot to be said for walking in faith and accepting deliverance too!

Now, I want to make sure you understand this: Anyone who would willingly give up his life for the gospel should be highly esteemed. I would never do or say anything to belittle a martyr's ultimate sacrifice for love of the Father.

Make no mistake, I don't love my life more than I love God. I'm not afraid to die if given the choice to renounce Him or be killed. If someone asked me if I loved Jesus while pointing a loaded gun in my face, I would say without hesitation, "Yes, I love Jesus." But according to this verse, it is my choice whether or not I am delivered from the death that could follow after taking that stand for the Lord—and I choose not to let someone take my life away from me!

We know from the writings of the early church fathers that many of the saints of the early church lived long, fruitful lives and then chose to be martyred. The Apostle Paul is one of those who did that. His enemies couldn't kill him when they wanted to. He lived until he had finished his course.

Paul even argued with himself about whether or not he wanted to go home to be with the Lord. He told the Philippian church, "I don't know if it's better to stay here or better to go. I know it's better for you if I stay, but it is far better for me if I go." (Philippians 1:23,24.)

Paul was actually debating with himself about whether or not he should lay down his life in martyrdom: *Do I let them do this to me? Or do I stay here and keep working for the kingdom of God?* Apparently, he had a choice, and he knew it!

Why do you think Paul just slung off that poisonous viper that had attached itself to his hand? (Acts 28:3-5.) Because he had a choice. Paul wasn't ready to go, and he knew that his flesh wasn't under subjection to the dangers of the world. He knew he had a choice. So he just flung off the viper and kept going about his business. It was no big deal because he knew that it was his choice whether or not he died and went to heaven at that time in his life.

Finally, Paul decided, *Okay, I've finished my course now. It's time to go home.* Only then was he martyred. Paul earned a martyr's crown, but he also lived out his life until he was finished with his divine assignment. Martyrdom was just the way he chose to go.

Just think what would have happened if Paul had chosen martyrdom early in his life. We wouldn't have half the New Testament!

Remember, 1 John 4:17 says **herein is our love made perfect that we may have boldness in the day of judgment: because as He is, so are we in this world.** He said in John 10:17-18 that it was His choice whether or not He gave His life for mankind:

> **Therefore doth my Father love me, because I lay down my life, that I might take it again. No man taketh it from me, but I lay it down of myself. I have power to lay it down, and I have power to take it again. This commandment have I received of my Father.**

Jesus could have called 10,000 angels to deliver Him (and if He could have done that, so can we!). He had a choice whether to pick up His life or lay it down.

So please understand, I'm not demeaning the martyrs. Throughout the centuries and still today, Christians all over the world have continued to give their lives for the furtherance of the gospel. When faced with denying Jesus or losing their lives, they choose the higher life. You would make the same choice if necessary. God's strength would rise in you to do so and without fear. I honor and esteem those believers. They were willing to lay down their lives in order to stay true to Jesus. God doesn't take the spilling of His people's blood lightly, and neither do I.

But even so, I want to tell you that *you can choose* whether or not you are supernaturally protected. For instance, suppose God asked you to go to China. If your uncle was martyred for the gospel in that country years ago, it might be a little difficult for you to say, "Yes, Lord, I'll take my family to China." If you are not absolutely assured that God is going to take care of you and your loved ones, you can't confidently go forth to fulfill His call.

But once you understand that you have a choice, you can boldly obey the Lord. You can go wherever God wants you to go and do whatever He wants you to do.

Yes, you can choose to be martyred. But you don't have to! In the face of death, you can keep your family safe. You can *know* that you and your children are protected because you have chosen to act on your faith in the blood of Jesus.

Now, some people may point out that God has often used the testimony of a believer who is martyred to bring others into His kingdom. That certainly is true. But, personally, I don't feel called to be a martyr. I'm receiving deliverance! My desire is to finish what God has called me to do. I can affect the kingdom of God while I'm still here on this earth!

Why Do Christians Get Caught in Bad Situations?

Knowing that you have a choice in this matter of divine protection may help you understand why Christians sometimes get caught in bad situations. This one question has gotten a lot of Christians confused about whether or not they can trust God to protect them.

So let's talk about that. Why *do* Christians get caught in bad situations? Well, first of all, let me say this one more time: *Protection is not automatic.*

Now, protection *would* be automatic if there wasn't an enemy trying to take it away from us every day. God doesn't want us to have to struggle or work for the benefits He has provided for us.

If the devil wasn't out there, there wouldn't be any earth-quakes, train accidents, shootings or disease. Protection would be ours whether we exercised our faith in the blood of Jesus or not.

But the devil *is* out there, and he never stops trying to take away our covenant blessings. That means we have to *lay hold* of our right to divine protection by standing in faith on God's Word and by pleading the blood of Jesus over our families every day.

Just consider this: Suppose you have hundreds of dollars in cash, and you decide to go walking through the worst part of town with some of that money hanging out in plain sight.

Well, it is very likely that you won't make it home with your money. Why is that? Because you didn't do anything to put yourself in a position of safety. You didn't properly secure your cash in a way that would protect it. Anyone who wants it can come along, rip it out of your pocket and run off with it. The money would still be yours, but because you didn't protect it, you would lose out on its benefits.

That's a good picture of what you are *not* supposed to do with God's promise of protection. You have to choose to secure it by acting in faith on the power of the blood. Otherwise, the devil may come along and steal it from you.

Second, I will say it again, we need to understand that *just because something happened doesn't mean it was God's will.* God gave us His will. It is found in the pages of the Bible. But that divine will isn't going to be fulfilled in our lives automatically.

Requirements for Protection

So what are those things God requires that we do in order to escape the judgment that is present in this world? We must choose to follow God's will; do the things He says we must do to be protected; and be obedient to His Word.

And as I said before, we must also listen to our spirits. For instance, we must refuse to go where we're not supposed to be. If God tweaks our spirits and says in that small, quiet voice, "Don't do that," we're supposed to listen and obey. That is so important to our own safety and to the safety of our children. We make things so much easier in our lives when we listen! As a mother, I'm always on the lookout for situations in which to teach this to my children.

Above all, we must take advantage of the power in the blood of Jesus, pleading His blood over our children every day. When we do that, we are building a hedge around our families through which judgment, death and tragedy cannot come.

First Peter 5:8 says, **Be sober, be vigilant; because your adversary the devil, as a roaring lion, walketh about,**

seeking whom he may devour. If you will live according to these principles I've been sharing with you, you won't be one of those whom the devil can devour.

Satan is looking for people who aren't living according to their blood covenant with God, people whose ears are not open to His voice. Those are the devil's favorite kind of people! I think he likes passive Christians more than he does his own sinners. He knows he can blast those Christians' lives, steal their children, kill half of them and then convince them that it was all God's doing. The devil gets a perverse pleasure out of that strategy! He hates God and he hates you.

But Satan isn't going to get any pleasure out of *my* family! We are off limits to him. I have already determined that no calamity will befall our home. I have laid hold of the power in the blood, and you can do the same for *your* family!

Build Up the Covenant Inside of You

Many times as you plead the blood of Jesus on a daily basis, the circumstances surrounding you will change. But more than anything else, the practice of pleading the blood changes *you*.

Pleading the blood isn't some magical incantation that you do to keep the devil from hurting your family. It is the way you lay hold of God's promise of protection. As you plead the blood of Jesus, you are fortifying your spirit with words of faith. You are making your stand against the devil. You are changing your thought processes. You are solidifying and building up your covenant with God on the inside. That firm foundation in His love drives out fear.

Then even when the devil tries to strike with one of his strategies against you or your family, you react the way the Word tells you to. You immediately speak deliverance according to the blood covenant you have with God.

Make it your goal to become covenant-minded in every area of life. Begin to see every obstacle you face through the eyes of your blood covenant.

For instance, if your child becomes sick, don't just see him through the eyes of your mind, will or emotions. If you do, your child will stay sick. Instead, respond according to the covenant you have with God. That covenant will reflect light on the situation, and you'll suddenly say, "Hey, this is not in my covenant with God! Jesus purchased my child's healing with the stripes on His back and with His blood! I claim total healing for my child's body in the Name of Jesus!"

That's why the heart of a covenant-minded believer is fixed as in Psalm 112, no matter what challenges may arise in life. He has his eyes on the covenant and not on the situation. He knows that his covenant says God will deliver him, so he just stays in faith, pleads the blood of Jesus and waits to see the outcome of his desire on the enemy.

When you plead the blood of Jesus every day, you are building the covenant strong and solid on the inside of you. Then when the pressure is on and you find you or your loved ones in a difficult situation, God's Word, our blood covenant, is what comes out of your mouth to deliver you.

For instance, I know of a covenant-minded woman who was in a bank when it was held up by thieves. The bank robbers made the people lay on the floor. Then they put guns to their heads and methodically began to shoot them one by one.

But when one of the robbers came to this one woman, she said boldly, "The blood of Jesus is against you!"

The man snarled, "I don't know what's going on, but I can't shoot you!" Then he moved on to the next victim and continued his horrible task.

Long before this tragedy occurred, that woman had been building the covenant on the inside by making a practice of pleading the blood of Jesus. And when death stared her in the face, it was her choice to be delivered.

It's your choice as well. It's also your children's choice. For instance, if your teenager ever found himself in a situation where someone at school stuck a gun in his face and asked him if he loved Jesus, he could say, "I plead the blood of Jesus!" He could choose to be delivered.

But that kind of faith-filled response doesn't come just because your child has heard about the blood of Jesus once in a while in a Sunday school teaching. It comes after you have helped him build a solid foundation of the blood covenant in his heart and have pled the blood of Jesus over him day after day after day.

Every night in our home, we plead the blood over our children as we tuck them in. Then they pray as well, and their prayers are every bit as powerful as mine are. They say, "I plead the blood of Jesus. No weapon formed against me shall prosper!"

My children know how to plead the blood. They may not yet fully understand everything I'm sharing with you in this book, but it's very real to them that they are protected. They are learning, they are building the blood covenant strong on the inside, even while they're young. And should they ever be alone when faced with an attack of the enemy, that covenant will come out of their mouths to deliver them and keep them safe!

A Testimony of Deliverance by the Blood

I can speak from personal experience about the value of building the blood covenant on the inside of you before a demonic attack hits your family. On Christmas Day in 1995, my 11-year-old daughter Lyndsey was struck with an aggressive case of meningitis. It just came clear out of the blue. One day she was fine, and then suddenly she was very, very sick.

Meningitis is a very fast-acting disease. Many times a child can be happy and playing in the morning; yet before 24 hours have passed, he is dead. The antibiotics don't have a chance to work because the parents are unaware that the child is seriously sick until he is within minutes of dying.

Lyndsey started feeling sick with flu-like symptoms on Christmas Eve. By Christmas morning, she was feeling so bad that she didn't want to come downstairs and open presents. My husband and I prayed over her and then went downstairs to share Christmas with the rest of the family. We didn't know Lyndsey was dangerously ill.

Then about 12:30 in the afternoon, we heard a screeching cry coming from Lyndsey's bedroom. We ran upstairs and found her screaming and thrashing on her bed, delirious. She didn't recognize anyone. Mystified, I thought, *Well, she was vomiting last night. Maybe her electrolytes are off.*

We called the doctor, and he said, "Take her to the hospital right away." By the time we arrived there, Lyndsey was totally unconscious. Her pupils were fixed and dilated, and she was as white as a sheet.

The medical staff took one look at her and rushed her past all the waiting patients into the emergency treatment area. Then they conducted a spinal tap, a procedure that entails taking fluid out of the patient's spinal column. If the fluid is clear, that is good news for the patient. If it is cloudy, that means the antibodies to fight meningitis are present. This is the way doctors determine whether or not a person has the disease.

I was standing near the doctor when he showed Lyndsey's spinal fluid to a nurse. The nurse remarked, "That's the cloudiest fluid I've ever seen!" That was a frightening thing for a mother to hear about her little girl!

The doctor then turned to me and said solemnly, "Your daughter has meningitis."

As soon as the doctor spoke those words, I felt as if someone had thrown a blanket of fear over me. That is the only way I know how to describe it. As that spirit of fear came on me, I could literally feel it trying to paralyze my own spirit.

Instead of responding to the doctor's words, I just turned around and left the room. He may have thought I was nuts, but right then I didn't know or care what anyone thought.

At that time, I didn't really know what meningitis was. I had read in the newspaper that several instances of children contracting meningitis had occurred in the community over the past couple of months, and I knew those children had died. And although I didn't know how far the disease had run its course in Lyndsey, I could see that the doctors were treating her with a very intense air of urgency.

When I walked out into the hall, my sister came over to me and asked, "What is it?"

But before I could answer her, there was something I had to do. Let me point out here that I was *not* thinking. Because I was living in the Holy of Holies I was responding in wisdom. I said, with a determined force that came from within, "I refuse fear!" Immediately, that blanket of fear lifted and left as if it were a whipped puppy. From that point on, I was able to operate on *God's* terms, not on fear's terms. Thank God for my parents who taught me to never let fear have its way.

Then I said, "Jesus, there is blood between me and You over Lyndsey. I have a covenant!"

For the rest of the ordeal with Lyndsey, I never had to deal with that kind of fear again. If a fearful thought tried to enter my mind, I was able to easily brush it away.

Later everyone said, "Oh, you must have been terrified." But I wasn't. I had total confidence that the Lord would deliver my daughter.

Why was it that easy for us to deal with fear in such a life-and-death situation? Well, Lyndsey got sick about two and a half years after my cousin Nikki died. For those two and a half years, my husband Win and I had been daily pleading the blood of Jesus over our family, building the covenant strong in our spirits.

I truly believe it was this two years of pleading the blood of Jesus that prepared us for this crisis. Because our covenant was so established in our hearts, the enemy was defeated. I am so thankful that God lets us know what we need before we need it!

If Win and I had responded as people of the world, our daughter would have gone the way of that disease and died. But because we knew we are not of this world—because we had built a hedge around our children by the blood—God was able to heal and deliver Lyndsey completely.

Declaring my covenant in that time of trouble was not something I had thought up beforehand. There wasn't time to run grab some tapes and read the Word to get strong in the Spirit. What is inside you will come out in an emergency— good or bad. The reality of my covenant with God rose up on the inside of me and armed me for the battle.

I didn't know all I know now about the blood, but what I did know had changed me. Every day for more than two years, I had reaffirmed my faith in the covenant, pleading the blood of Jesus and speaking God's promises for my family. That daily exercise of reminding myself and the enemy that my family was covered by the blood had built the covenant strong inside my spirit. And when I needed that covenant to take effect, it rose up and determined the words of my mouth, causing me to do and say the right things when it mattered the most.

I didn't have to stand there and think, *Okay, now, what am I supposed to say and do in a situation like this?* In fact, because your mind shuts down (Praise God!) you can't do that. This is a perfect example of Matthew 12:34-35.

> **Oh generation of vipers, how can ye, being evil, speak good things? For out of the abundance of the heart the mouth speaketh. As good man out of the good treasure of the heart bringeth forth good things: and an evil man out of the evil treasure bringeth forth evil things.**

When you get under pressure what is inside you *will* come out—good or bad. And if the Word is not in you when trouble comes, it won't come out.

The blood covenant within me literally *propelled* those words of faith out of my mouth without my having to think about it at all. I love the *Amplified* version of verse 35. It says, **The good man from his inner good treasure *flings* forth good things.** Well, my spirit started flinging! This disease had no right to my daughter's body!

At about 3:30 in the afternoon, the doctor started Lyndsey on strong antibiotics. However, he warned us not to get our hopes up. "Meningitis is very deadly," he told us. "We have antibiotics to fight the disease, but these antibiotics take at least 24 to 48 hours to have any kind of effect, and children who have contracted meningitis usually die before 24 hours have passed."

Remember, Lyndsey started feeling sick on Christmas Eve, so she had already been sick with this disease for 24 hours. That meant by the time we reached the hospital, the disease had almost reached the final stages of progression— a process that normally ended in death.

I was quickly learning what a fast-acting, evil disease meningitis is. All sickness and disease is evil, but this one has the devil's signature handwritten all over it. People who contract the disease and survive can lose their hearing, limbs— even their mental ability.

According to the doctor, something had to change quickly in Lyndsey's condition or she would die. When Win and I calmly told him that Jesus died on the cross so that she didn't have to die from this, he looked at us and said, "I can agree with that." You know he didn't know what he was saying, but God caused him to be in agreement.

This brings up another important point. When people are not established in their covenant, they are afraid of the doctor's report. Remember Psalm 112? Even Christians can fall into that category of the wicked if they have an evil heart of unbelief. I've seen people yell at the doctor, telling him they won't receive that report—then they launch into their confessions and hurl them in his face.

What's the problem here? The problem (and the killer) is they are not doing these actions out of faith in their covenant with God, but out of fear that it won't work this time. All they get from it is an angry doctor and a firm foundation of fear. You cannot wage spiritual warfare out of fear. And you cannot operate in fear and faith simultaneously because fear and faith take up the same spiritual space.

Well, about 8:00 that evening, Jerry and Carolyn Savelle came to the hospital to be with us (my parents were out of town at the time). While my husband stayed with Lyndsey, I went with the Savelles, my sister and my brother-in-law (who are our pastors) to the hospital chapel to take Communion and just settle the matter in my heart. I didn't know it at the time, but my parents were doing the very same thing at the very same minute. They were over 800 miles away!

Now, we weren't just trying to be religious or to impress God by taking Communion. We were remembering that

Jesus shed His blood to bring our blood covenant with God to pass. So we set before us the Scriptures that promised us Lyndsey's healing. Then we partook of the Communion elements, knowing in our hearts that she was well and whole because the Bible said it was so.

There is so much power in taking Communion. It seals your faith in the covenant you have already built up inside yourself by pleading the blood of Jesus each day.

As we sat there taking Communion, Brother Savelle received a word from the Lord: *"As suddenly as this has come on her, it is going to go."* So when I left that chapel, there was no doubt in my mind that we had won. No weapon formed against my daughter could prosper.

I have to share with Win what just happened, I thought. But before I could reenter Lyndsey's room, I had to go through a complicated sterilization procedure, necessary because of the highly contagious nature of the disease. By the time I had put on all the hospital garb and carefully washed, about 15 minutes had passed.

When I was ready, I walked into Lyndsey's hospital room—only to find her talking to Win. When I had left to go to the chapel a short time before, she had been both unconscious and delirious. To keep her from harming herself as she thrashed about, the medical staff had tied her to her bed.

Lyndsey hadn't been able to say a word that made sense since we had gotten to the hospital. It had been less than five hours since she started taking antibiotics. Yet here she was, talking to her dad.

Overcome with joy, I asked, "What happened?"

Win explained: "Lyndsey was just lying there unconscious, but about 15 minutes ago she turned her head to look at me and said, 'Merry Christmas, Daddy.' Then she asked me, 'What are all these machines?' So I've been explaining to her what has been going on!"

Just like that, Lyndsey was in her right mind again. From that moment on, her recovery was miraculously rapid. It wasn't the antibiotics the doctor gave her; there hadn't been enough time for the medicine to take effect. It was the healing power of God at work in my daughter's body that had turned the situation around.

By the time my parents had flown back home, arriving at the hospital about midnight that night, Lyndsey was talking to all of us. She was having to use her faith for her head to stop hurting and for every symptom to go, but she was well on her way back to complete wholeness.

The next morning, one of the doctors came in to check on Lyndsey and was shocked to see that she was still alive, much less on her way to total recovery. The doctor had just seen the test results, which indicated that Lyndsey had contracted the deadliest form of meningitis. Children just didn't live long after contracting this particular virus.

It still had not been 24 hours since Lyndsey had been put on antibiotics. But at 8:00 that morning, she was ordered out of intensive care into a private room. I guarantee you, only the blood of Jesus and the Word of God can do that.

Lessons Learned

I want to give you a few thoughts about what I learned through this situation with my daughter. First, one of the main passages of Scripture we stood on during the entire experience was Isaiah 54. As I mentioned before, there are some powerful covenant promises in that chapter. Let me show you just a few of them:

> **And all thy children shall be taught of the Lord; and great shall be the peace of thy children. In righteousness shalt thou be established: thou shalt be far from oppression; for thou shalt not fear: and from terror; for it shall not come near thee.**
>
> **Behold, they shall surely gather together, but not by me: whosoever shall gather together against thee shall fall for thy sake.**

Behold, I have created the smith that bloweth the coals in the fire, and that bringeth forth an instrument for his work; and I have created the waster that destroys.

No weapon that is formed against thee shall prosper; and every tongue that shall rise against thee in judgment thou shalt condemn. This is the heritage of the servants of the Lord, and their righteousness is of me, saith the Lord.

Isaiah 54:13-17

Verse 15 says, **I have created the waster to destroy.** That doesn't mean God created the devil to destroy. We know from the Word that when God created Lucifer, he was perfect. (Ezekiel 28:12.) The literal Hebrew says that God created the waster that destroys, and He is saying in this verse, "I created him, and I can handle him."

God knows how to take care of the devil, and He is on our side. Therefore, we must give Him full freedom to thwart the enemy's attacks on our family and keep him out of our lives.

Then in verse 17, it says, **Every tongue that shall rise against thee in judgment thou shalt condemn.** Every day, the accuser of the brethren has his finger in your face, trying to condemn you with his evil judgments, such as, "You're sick. You're poor. I'm going to hurt your children today." But according to verse 17, we can condemn the devil's accusations against us. How do we do that? By pleading the blood.

These verses in Isaiah 54 were some of the Scriptures my husband and I had used to build a covenant hedge of protection around our family for more than two years. We weren't standing in our own righteousness as we claimed these promises for Lyndsey. We were standing in Jesus' righteousness by virtue of His blood. And as we declared in faith that no weapon formed against Lyndsey would prosper, God delivered her from imminent death and restored her to total wholeness.

Here's another important point to understand: It wasn't because I am Kenneth and Gloria Copeland's daughter that God came through for Lyndsey. It was the fact that we know who we are in Jesus and in His blood that made the difference.

In the same way, it doesn't matter who you are. It doesn't matter if you are famous or unknown. It doesn't matter if you are from a rich family or a poor family. A lot of money can get you a lot of things, but if you are sick and there is no earthly cure for your condition, you need to start doing things *God's* way. Money is a very poor source when it comes to healing, joy, peace or anything else for that matter.

Finally, I want to share with you something else I learned through this whole situation. I discovered firsthand how

God makes allowances for the times we miss it as we daily plead the blood of Jesus over our lives.

The Lord had been talking to me about taking Communion with my family on that particular Christmas Eve. I had even bought all the Communion supplies to do it.

However, at the Christmas Eve family gathering, I was so busy enjoying our time together that I forgot what the Lord had told me to do. It wasn't until everyone was starting to leave that I said, "Oh, we forgot to take Communion." But given the lateness of the hour and the fact that some family members were almost out the door, I decided, *Well, we'll just take Communion together next Christmas Eve.*

That was a big mistake. After the entire ordeal with Lyndsey was over and she was back home again, the Lord spoke these words to my spirit: "If you had done what I said that night, you wouldn't have gone through this."

God wasn't trying to start a new tradition in our family when He impressed me to take Communion together on Christmas Eve. He had a specific purpose for it. But I missed it when I took His prompting too lightly and decided to forego the family time of Communion for the sake of convenience.

My family could have bypassed that entire ordeal. We could have had a peaceful, healthy Christmas. Nevertheless, because I had faithfully pled the blood of Jesus over my family and built the covenant strong in my heart, God delivered my daughter out of a deadly situation. And it ended up being a great Christmas after all.

You build a firm foundation for yourself when you plead the blood of Jesus every day. Then each day and month and year that you keep pleading the blood of Jesus, you put new layers on that foundation until the covenant is built solid and strong on the inside of you.

That's so important, because someday a devilish attack may come like the one I faced with Lyndsey. In times like that, you don't have time to get ready to take a stance of faith by meditating on some Scriptures. You have to respond right the first time, or the devil wins the battle.

That's why you must keep building up the covenant in your spirit, pleading the blood of Jesus over your family day after day. Don't wait until problems arise to start building that covenant inside of you. That would be like starting to build your house the night before a hurricane hits! No, you build your house when it isn't storm season. You build it strong on a solid foundation so that when the storms hit, nothing can knock it down.

It's the same way in the spiritual realm. If you have built a strong foundation of your covenant in your heart, you will respond in the right way when pressure comes. Words of faith in God's covenant promises will come out of your mouth, bringing His power on the scene and giving you the victory.

But it is your choice. You have to choose to lay hold of your covenant of protection with God. The protection is there if you want it, but you don't have to take it. You can choose to get caught in a bad situation and let the enemy send you or your child on an early ride to heaven. *Or* you can lay hold of your protection by standing on God's Word and boldly pleading the blood of the Lamb.

CHAPTER 7

It Matters Where You Live

So if it's your choice whether or not to be delivered, what is that choice hinging on? The answer is simple: *It matters where you live.* That is the key. The reason you plead the blood of Jesus is to put yourself and your children in the place where you are supposed to abide continually—the Holy of Holies.

I'm telling you, my friend, you make better decisions when you live in that place. You hear God's voice better. You walk in love better. And when you plead the blood of Jesus in the morning, you secure your place there.

What You Say Is Where You Live

Remember what I told you earlier: Your faith in the blood is executed and entered into by the words of your mouth. Why is what you say so important? *Because what you say is where you are going to live.*

If words of poverty, sickness and fear are coming out of your mouth, I can guarantee you that you are living in the natural realm with a lot of poverty, sickness and fear. But if your words are proclaiming healing, prosperity and protection by the blood of Jesus, then you're living in the Holy of Holies. Your natural circumstances may not have caught up with your confession of faith yet, but what you are saying is exactly where you are headed.

Look again at what Proverbs 12:13-14 AMP has to say about the connection between our words and divine protection:

> **The wicked is [dangerously] snared by the transgression of his lips, but the [uncompromisingly] righteous shall come out of trouble. From the fruit of his words a man shall be satisfied with good....**

Now, "the wicked man" referred to here is a person who isn't in covenant with God. However, the same principle applies to a person who doesn't *know* the covenant he has with God. Both will be dangerously snared by the transgression of their lips.

This explains why verse 21 AMP is true:

No [actual] evil, misfortune, or calamity shall
come upon the righteous, but the wicked shall
be filled with evil, misfortune, and calamity.

Think of these proverbs in light of what Moses said in
Deuteronomy 30:19.

I call heaven and earth to record this day
against you, that I have set before you life and
death, blessing and cursing: therefore *choose
life*, that both thou and thy seed may live.

It's very clear that where you live is your choice. You can
be one of the righteous who lives free of evil misfortune
and calamity, or you can place yourself in the same category
as "the wicked" and live a life filled with evil, misfortune
and calamity.

Sadly, there are too many Christians who are living on
that wicked side of life—not because they want to be wicked
or do evil things, but because they don't say or do what
God's Word says. They don't honor the blood of Jesus, so
their lives seem to be filled with one crisis after another.

But these people don't have to live with calamity and
misfortune. They could choose to pick up their Bible and
find out how to get out of their bad situation. They could dis-
cover for themselves that things go well in the lives of those
for whom the Word of God is the final authority.

The problem is that Christians who live on the wicked side of life don't give the Word any credence. "God didn't protect Grandma, so He won't protect me," they say. "Whatever happens is going to happen, and there is nothing I can do about it." And what they say is exactly where they end up living.

But these Christians are not honoring the Word with that attitude, because God says there *is* something they can do about it. They can apply the blood of Jesus to their lives with the words of their mouths.

Honor the Word

The key to living victoriously in this life is to become covenant-minded—to honor the blood of Jesus and the Word above everything else. That includes honoring the Word above your experiences, circumstances or what anyone else says. If your family doesn't agree with the Word of God, you should pray for them and walk in love with them, but always make sure that you *honor the Word*.

I've counseled people who just couldn't seem to grasp this basic, all-important concept. For instance, one woman whom I've often counseled comes crying to me with the same problem every time. At every counseling session, I sit down with this woman and ask, "Are you reading the Word?"

"Well, no," she replies. "I just..." and then gives me her latest excuse. Finally I told her, "Nothing is going to change in your life until you honor the Word and give it first place in your life. You have to come to the place where you say, 'My answers are in here, and I am determined to find them.'"

That is why the Word talks so much about the man whose heart is fixed and established. He is the one who honors, reveres and worships the Lord. (Psalm 112:7 AMP.)

If you revere the Lord and put Him first place in your life, you will go to His Word to find your answers. Then whatever the Word says to do, you will do it. You will consider the Bible as your instruction Book for life.

That is what makes you a covenant person whose heart is fixed. Nothing can move you off your stance of faith. Death no longer holds sway in your life.

I think Ecclesiastes 12:13 AMP says best what I'm trying to get across to you:

> **Now all has been heard; the end of the matter is: Fear God [revere and worship Him, knowing that He is] and keep His command-ments** [in other words, look to the Word as the end of all matters], **for this is the whole of man [the full, original purpose of his creation, the object of God's providence, the root of char-acter, the foundation of all happiness, the**

adjustment to all inharmonious circumstances and conditions under the sun] and the whole [duty] for every man.

Notice what this verse says about the Word of God. For one thing, it is *the root of character.* As you sink yourself into the Word and cement yourself in its truth, the Word becomes the root or the basis of your character. Character that is rooted in God's Word causes you to make the right choices and to do the right thing. However, this kind of godly character is only developed when you make the Word the end of all matters in your life.

The Word is also *the foundation of all happiness* and *the adjustment to all inharmonious circumstances and conditions under the sun.* If you have an inharmonious circumstance or condition in your life, your answer will be found in God's Word. As you honor God's Word and begin to seek wisdom in its pages, He will show you where your answer is.

The fact is, there isn't one thing the enemy can throw at you or your family that you can't overwhelmingly overcome when you honor the Word above all else in your life. That means if the devil tries to attack your children, he can't leave them with anything missing or broken. Otherwise, he has prospered in that attack, and Isaiah 54:17 says that *no* weapon formed against you will prosper. Nothing Satan can come up with is bigger, higher or more powerful than the Word of God and the blood of Jesus that ratified that Word.

Everything contained within the Bible was purchased for you by the blood of Jesus. Every promise in the Word belongs to you, and the devil can't do one thing about it, apart from what you allow him to do. He can't attack you or your children with any circumstance or condition that isn't answered in the Word of God.

You can overcome every demonic strategy against your family by honoring God's Word. Live by it, live on it, live in it. Remember—*it matters where you live.*

Learn how to live each day in the Holy of Holies by virtue of the blood of Jesus. Then when a challenge arises, come boldly before God's throne and ask Him to reveal to you in His Word the answer you need.

Once you have your answer, make sure your words always stay in line with what God has said on the matter. Your words of faith will not only guarantee your ultimate victory, but they will make sure you retain your current living status in the Holy of Holies.

Don't Be an 'Earth-Inhabiter'

Revelation 12:10-12 has more to say about where believers are supposed to dwell during their lives on this earth:

And I heard a loud voice saying in heaven, Now is come salvation, and strength, and the

> kingdom of our God, and the power of his Christ: for the accuser of our brethren is cast down, which accused them before our God day and night.
>
> And they overcame him by the blood of the Lamb, and by the word of their testimony; and they loved not their lives unto the death.
>
> Therefore rejoice, ye heavens, and ye that dwell in them. Woe to the inhabiters of the earth and of the sea! for the devil is come down unto you, having great wrath, because he knoweth that he hath but a short time.
>
> Revelation 12:10-12

Verse 12 tells us where we are today in God's timeline. In the past few years, tragic calamities have escalated more than ever before. We don't even live in the same world now as we did 20 years ago. The devil knows his time is short, and he is upset about it. He is desperate. Therefore, he is roaming the earth, trying to do everything he can to stop the inevitable victory of the Body of Christ.

But what happens to you and your family depends on where you dwell. If you dwell in the heavens, or in the Holy of Holies, God tells you to rejoice because you have overcome. You are one of those who comes boldly before the throne of grace by the blood of Jesus to receive everything you need.

But inhabiters of the earth are going to experience calamities and misfortunes. The Bible says, "Woe to them!"

Too many children of God are still inhabiting the earth. That's why we are seeing so many good Christians taken out by the enemy through tragic circumstances.

These Christians become part of the earth-dwellers' woe because they choose to inhabit the earth instead of inhabiting their covenant in the Holy of Holies. They live their lives trusting in the world's system and their own wisdom and ability. They certainly aren't trusting in God's ways. The devil has convinced them that God won't protect them. The enemy has even succeeded in convincing some of them that *God* is their problem. Because these people allow Satan to deceive them, they become earth-inhabiters, subject to the same calamities that other people in the world suffer through.

But the truth is, that is their choice. The Word has the answers they need to become "Holy of Holies dwellers" and to overcome the enemy's strategies in their lives if they would just choose to honor what God says above all else.

The Blood and Our Words

Verse 11 says that heaven-dwellers overcome the enemy **by the blood of the Lamb, and by the word of their testimony.**

Notice that there are two parts to this verse. As a heaven-dweller, you overcome the devil's strategies against your family by the blood of Jesus *and* by the word of your testimony.

As we have discussed before, nothing in the Word comes without declaring it, laying hold of it and speaking it forth in faith. After all, when you were born again, you had to confess Jesus as your Savior. In the same way, the blood of the Lamb won't deliver you unless you lay hold of it with the words of your mouth.

So we know we are living in the last days. The earth is filling up with sin, judgment, tragedy and terrible circumstances because the wages of sin is death. However, Romans 5:20 says that where sin abounds, God's grace much more abounds. According to that Scripture, more grace is available to us now than ever before because sin is abounding more now than ever before.

The devil is mad. He knows his time is short and there isn't anything he can do about it. Therefore, he's plotting all sorts of evil things. Satan is going to try to take out as many people as he can, and Christians are the ones he would most like to get out of his way.

If you're not really doing anything to hurt the devil's kingdom, you might not be his main target. Nevertheless, you live on this earth in which sin and judgment abounds more and more. Just that fact alone puts you in danger if you decide to be an earth-inhabiter.

But he isn't touching my family because we are kingdom-dwellers, *not* earth-dwellers. Every morning we place ourselves under the protective covering of the blood of Jesus. We say, "We plead the blood of Jesus over our family this morning. Father, we dwell in the Holy of Holies today. We live our lives there. And we thank You, Lord, for the abundance of grace that we find there to protect, deliver and meet every need!"

You can make that same choice as well. Instead of being earth-inhabiters, you and your children can be kingdom-dwellers—untouchable by the enemy because of the power in the blood of the Lamb.

Dwelling in the Secret Place

You should understand by now that you can live your life in absolute certainty that God will protect you and your children from harm, no matter what is going on around you. But let's look at another important passage of Scripture to make sure that knowledge is rooted deep in your heart.

Psalm 91 is a chapter most Christians have stood on in faith at one time or another. But many of these same Christians think, *I have claimed that chapter for my family in times past, but it doesn't seem like we're living the full benefit of it. We haven't been delivered out of every attack of the enemy. Bad things have happened at times.*

Well, let's look a little closer at this chapter to find out why that is the case with so many Christians. Before we read it, however, let me stress again these two points: 1) It is important where you dwell in life; and 2) you are a citizen of heaven. By the blood of Jesus, you can dwell in the Holy of Holies even though you live here on this earth.

Now let's see what Psalm 91:1-4 AMP says:

> **He who dwells in the secret place of the Most High shall remain stable and fixed under the shadow of the Almighty [Whose power no foe can withstand].**
>
> **I will say of the Lord, He is my Refuge and my Fortress, my God; on Him I lean and rely, and in Him I [confidently] trust!**
>
> **For [then] He will deliver you from the snare of the fowler and from the deadly pestilence. [Then] He will cover you with His pinions, and under His wings shall you trust and find refuge; His truth and His faithfulness are a shield and a buckler.**

Notice that Psalm 91 is totally conditional. Two conditions are given in verse 1 and 2 that must be met first before the rest of the verses can be claimed. The first one is that you must *dwell in the secret place of God.*

The problem is, most Christians don't know *how* to dwell in the secret place. They think it is a nice phrase, but they aren't sure what it means. *Maybe we dwell in the secret place when we pray or go to church,* they think. But that just isn't so 100 percent of the time.

However, dwelling in the secret place is a totally reachable goal. The secret place is the Holy of Holies, the throne of grace. All these terms are talking about the same place, a secret place reserved only for God's people. The devil can't get in there. In the secret place of the Most High, you can live safe, healed and protected, abiding continually in the presence of God.

The second condition that must be fulfilled in order to enjoy the benefits of Psalm 91 is that you have to *say* something: **I will say of the Lord, He is my Refuge and my Fortress...in Him I [confidently] trust** (v. 2 AMP). Again, you can see the important role of the words you speak. You have to say with your mouth, "Lord, You are my refuge. I confidently trust You with my life and with my children!"

Once you meet these two conditions, all the other promises of protection in Psalm 91 are yours to claim for your family. Let's read on:

> **You shall not be afraid of the terror of the night, nor of the arrow (the evil plots and slanders of the wicked) that flies by day, nor of the pestilence that stalks in darkness, nor**

> of the destruction and sudden death that sur-
> prise and lay waste at noonday.
>
> > Psalm 91:5,6 AMP

These verses talk about **the evil plots and slanders of the wicked** and the **destruction and sudden death that surprise and lay waste at noonday.** That sounds like the kind of things we hear about on the news every night. But it doesn't matter what kind of evil plot the devil tries against you or your children; his strategies can't prosper. As verse 5 AMP says, **You shall not be afraid of the terror by night.**

That sounds like the covenant man we talked about earlier. He does not fear evil tidings because his heart is fixed on God and His Word.

Now look at what verses 7-8 AMP say:

> **A thousand may fall at your side, and ten thousand at your right hand, but it shall not come near you.**
>
> **Only a spectator shall you be [yourself inaccessible in the secret place of the Most High] as you witness the reward of the wicked.**

You are inaccessible to the enemy's strategies when you are in the secret place of the Most High.

The key is to live your life in that secret place. Jesus entered the secret place of the Most High, the Holy of Holies, by His own blood. Your access to the secret place is by virtue

of His blood as well. In that secret place, you and your children are inaccessible to the enemy **because you have made
the Lord your refuge, and the Most High your dwelling
place** (v. 9 AMP).

Now you can see why Psalm 91 hasn't been fulfilled in
many Christians' lives. They may have read it, quoted it, con-
fessed it and prayed it. But if they haven't done what Psalm
91 tells them to do, they are not eligible to receive God's
promise of protection for their families.

When the Lord first taught me how to fulfill His conditions so I could receive the promises contained in these
verses, I felt like He had given me a very precious gift. As a
wife and mother, I so appreciated that gift because now I can
be absolutely certain that my family is protected by the
blood of Jesus.

I am so thrilled to know that. It doesn't matter what God
asks me to do, I can do it boldly because I know He's going
to protect my family and me.

I know God will protect your family, too, if you'll just act
on these truths I'm sharing with you. I suggest that you read
this Psalm to your children every day so its promise of protection can be rooted deep in their hearts. As you read it, put
their names in the verses. Make it personal to them.

You and your children can be safe and secure, no matter
what is going on around them. Your part is to dwell in the

secret place of the Most High and to speak forth your trust in the Lord. As you do, God will be your family's Refuge and Fortress in every situation. Don't ever let the devil talk you out of that.

Finally, let me plant you one last Scripture in your heart to build your faith in God's protecting power. Psalm 33:18-19 AMP says, **Behold, the Lord's eye is upon those who fear Him [who revere and worship Him with awe], who wait for Him and hope in His mercy and loving-kindness, to deliver them from death and keep them alive in famine.**

It's all over the Word: You and your family can be protected and delivered if you will just receive and appropriate God's promise of protection. Your children can live in that supernatural protection 24 hours a day. You can have what the Word says you can have.

Just live every day the way God intended for you to live—covered in the blood of Jesus, clothed in His righteousness, endowed with His wisdom and abiding in His presence. From your position before the throne of grace, plead the blood of Jesus over yourself, your spouse and your children with the absolute, utter certainty that God will keep them safe.

Then with the words of your mouth, boldly declare your faith in the blood of Jesus:

"Although we live in a world that is overflowing with judgment and sin, we will find only peace, protection and abundant grace wherever we go. No weapon formed against us shall prosper, for the blood of Jesus delivers us from evil and protects us from all harm!"

As you pray the following prayer, remember to pray the same over yourself and your spouse. In fact, I include my grandmother in our daily prayer. She's protected by the blood too.

Begin to build the habit of praying like this every day. Ask the Lord to remind you and help you. He will. You may forget sometimes, but keep on. You'll begin to build your covenant on the inside of you. Ask the Lord to never allow you to let these things slip.

And, you and your family too will live your lives from the Holy of Holies—protected, secure, safe and in His peace.

Prayer of Protection
for Your Family

Father, I thank You for Your covenant promise of protection. Right now I call upon the covenant I have with You and plead the blood of Jesus over my husband/wife, my children and myself.

Angels, I charge you to watch over my family and me to protect us, for we are walking in the footsteps of Jesus. Go before us, behind us, beside us and all the way around us. Keep us from calamity, evil and misfortune. (I name all of our names to the Lord.)

No evil will befall my family in the Name of Jesus! No weapon formed against them will prosper, and every lying tongue that rises up against them I do condemn, for this is my heritage as a servant of the Lord.

I thank You, Father, that great is the peace of my children. Their righteousness is of You. They don't walk in their own righteousness, but in Your righteousness by the blood of Jesus. I thank You for that, Lord. They will not get off track in life, none of their steps shall slide (Psalm 37:31) for Your Holy Spirit will guide them every step of the way.

Father, Your Word says that we, Your sheep, know Your voice. It says You will show us things to come. It says the voice of Your Spirit will come to us and say, "This is the way; walk in it." I stand on these promises, Lord, and ask that You teach us to hear Your voice. Help us recognize when You are speaking to us, and we will obey.

Now I stand in Your holy of holies and open my spirit to receive the wisdom You have afforded me. I put myself in a position to hear and receive instruction from You. I enter the secret place of the Most High by the blood of the Lamb, and I purpose to live my life in Your presence.

I thank You that You are faithful to Your Word, Father. I thank You that what You say is certain and sure. When You say You will deliver us, we can rely on that promise. So right now I receive Your supernatural protection and deliverance for my family and me in Jesus' Name. Amen.

About the Author

Speaker, author, musician, wife, and mother of four, Kellie Copeland Kutz has played a major role in bringing the gospel to those hungry for the truth of God's Word. Kellie has taken the Word of God to the world through television, print media, and conferences, as well as her music ministry.

Kellie directs the development of all Kenneth Copeland Ministries' children's product, and is the contributing editor for *Shout! The Voice of Victory for Kids*, a bimonthly children's magazine with more than 160,000 subscriptions. She is best known as *Commander Kellie*—the fearless, faith-filled adventurer in the *Commander Kellie and the SuperKids*sm video and audio series and *Commander Kellie and the SuperKids*sm novels.

Like her character, Kellie has a heart for all to know victory in life is achieved through a close and personal relationship with God, the Father.

Kellie has an extensive music ministry, inspired by her father, television and conference minister, Kenneth Copeland. Her musical accomplishments include a solo album, *Refreshing Times;* a duet album with Scott Johnson, *Goodbye World;* and three children's albums, *Precious Moments, Lullabies,* and her newest project, *And Jesus Healed Them All,* a children's healing music album.

Kellie and her husband, Win, the director of Kenneth Copeland Ministries' music department, have four children, Rachel, Lyndsey, Jenny, and Max.

Kellie says, "My desire is to see people live on the Word." She gets excited when she sees someone who has heard the Word, put action with it, and lives a victorious life.

To contact Kellie Copeland Kutz,
write:

Kenneth Copeland Ministries
Fort Worth, Texas 76192
United States of America

*Please include your prayer requests
and comments when you write.*

Prayer of Salvation

A born-again, committed relationship with God is the key to a victorious life. Jesus, the Son of God, laid down His life and rose again so that we could spend eternity with Him in heaven and experience His absolute best on earth. The Bible says, "For God so loved the world, that he gave his only begotten Son, that whosoever believeth in him should not perish, but have everlasting life" (John 3:16).

It is the will of God that everyone receive eternal salvation. The way to receive this salvation is to call upon the name of Jesus and confess Him as your Lord. The Bible says, "That if thou shalt confess with thy mouth the Lord Jesus, and shalt believe in thine heart that God hath raised him from the dead, thou shalt be saved. For whosoever shall call upon the name of the Lord shall be saved" (Rom. 10:9,13).

Jesus has given salvation, healing, and countless benefits to all who call upon His name. These benefits can be yours if you receive Him into your heart by praying this prayer:

Heavenly Father, I come to You admitting that I am a sinner. Right now, I choose to turn away from sin, and I ask You to cleanse me of all unrighteousness. I believe that Your Son, Jesus, died on the cross to take away my sins. I also believe that He rose again from the dead so that I may be justified and made righteous through faith in Him. I call upon the name of Jesus Christ to be the Savior and Lord of my life. Jesus, I choose to follow You, and I ask that You fill me with the power of the Holy Spirit. I declare right now that I am a born-again child of God. I am free from sin, and full of the righteousness of God. I am saved in Jesus' name, amen.

If you have prayed this prayer to receive Jesus Christ as your Savior, or if this book has changed your life, we would like to hear from you. Please write us at:

Harrison House Publishers
P.O. Box 35035
Tulsa, Oklahoma 74153

You can also visit us on the Web at
www.harrisonhouse.com

Additional copies of this book
are available from your local bookstore
or from:

HARRISON HOUSE
P. O. Box 35035
Tulsa, Oklahoma 74153

The Harrison House Vision

Proclaiming the truth and the power
Of the Gospel of Jesus Christ
With excellence;

Challenging Christians to
Live victoriously,
Grow spiritually,
Know God intimately.